# Beginner's
# IRISH

# Beginner's
# IRISH

Gabriel Rosenstock

HIPPOCRENE BOOKS
*New York*

For information, address:
Hippocrene Books, Inc.
171 Madison Avenue
New York, NY 10016

ISBN 0-7818-0784-0

Cataloging in Publication data available from the Library of Congress.

Printed in the United States of America.

# Contents

# A Brief History of the Irish Language

The Irish language has been spoken on the island of Ireland for the past two and a half thousand years. Is this not reason enough to study it and to strive for its survival? Irish belongs to the Celtic family of languages. Its root language was *Indo-European*, that is to say, the language of Eastern Europe and Western Asia spoken towards the end of the *Stone Age*, some four thousand years ago, and which began to split up into the prototypes of most of today's European languages, among the exceptions being *Basque, Finnish and Hungarian*.

As to *Indo-European*? We know that the Hindu system of law is strikingly similar to ancient Irish law. Parallels also exist between *Old Irish* and *Sanskrit*, not only in root words but in metrics as well. Ireland's sacred river, the *Boyne*, is linguistically cognate with *Govinda* or Krishna. *Uttar* Pradesh in India finds its echo in Irish *uachtar*, upper part.

In *The Celtic Realms* by Myles Dillon and Nora Chadwick (Weidenfeld & Nicolson, 1972) we read:

> The oldest narrative form in Indo-European tradition seems to have been a prose narrative, with dialogue in verse. The verse was metrically fixed and unchanging, but the prose was left to the creative memory of the storyteller. This was the oldest Indian form, as found in the Buddhist Jātakas and in a few examples even in the ancient Brāhmanas of the Vedic period. It was also the Irish form; and it appears in some of the oral epics of Central Asia. The Irish sagas are in prose, but when a champion claims his right to the Hero's Portion [of a pig], he speaks in verse; when Deirdre says farewell to Scotland and when she laments the death of her lover, she speaks in verse. In India, and presumably in Greece, this ancient form developed into epic poetry, so that in the Mahābhārata and

Rāmāyana, and in Homer, we have long narrative poems. But in Ireland the old Indo-European form survived into the Middle Ages, providing another example of the great archaism of Irish tradition ...

Celtic languages in use today are *Irish, Scottish Gaelic, Welsh* and *Breton. Manx*—the Gaelic of the Isle of Man—and *Cornish* died, though attempts are being made to revive them. Of the four living Celtic languages, opinions vary as to which is the strongest. Some would argue they are all doomed, others take a more optimistic view. Factors which might color the argument, one way or the other, include the number of young native speakers and their pattern of language usage, the position and relative importance of the language in first, second and third-level educational institutions, the strength of the language in terms of book publishing, the quality of its literature and how it is perceived, the use of language in film, radio, television, popular entertainment, journalism, its use in the home, its use in the political, business, commercial and religious life of the country, the attitude towards it as expressed by opinion formers, as well as its symbolic strength as a badge of nationhood or cultural distinctiveness.

No one language will come out tops in all categories but it is likely that those in the know would deem Welsh to be the strongest and Breton the weakest of the four. There are roughly 500 languages, many of them in North and South America—which are on the death list. Not one of them will survive—short of a miracle. Can the Celtic languages escape the same fate, even with concerted language planning, strong government leadership and a galvanization of human will and resources? It may well be that to ensure the survival of minority languages, we may need consciousness-raising on a global scale, such as we now have in relation to the environment, so that the globalization of culture, generally, is fitted with an inbuilt health warning not to obliterate what is unique and different on its relentless path.

## THE CONTINENTAL CELTS

Linguists refer to Irish as the *Goidelic* branch of insular Celtic and further distinguish Irish by a hard C or Q sound as opposed to the P sound of our Welsh neighbors. If we are the insular Celts, who were the

*Continental Celts?* We know quite a lot about them from Roman and Greek commentaries and from archaeological research. The two periods of early and late Iron Age culture are named after important sites, *Hallstatt* (800-450 B.C.) after a site in Austria, and *La Tène (500-50 B.C.)* after a site in Switzerland (the name means "the shallows" and "tanaí" is modern Irish for "shallow"). The extent of the Celtic realm of influence can best be imagined by naming a number of Celtic settlements: *Bonn, Belgrade, Budapest, Ankara, London, Lyon, Strasbourg, Paris, Geneva,* and *Vienna.* They may have largely disappeared from the map of the world, but the Celts resurrect themselves—Riverdance-fashion—every so often. Napoleon went to battle with a copy of Ossian—even if that book was a bit of a forgery.

Long forgotten, the Celts came to the fore spectacularly in 1846 when excavations in *Hallstatt*, in the Salzkammergut (salt mines) region of Austria, unearthed two thousand Iron Age graves, long-lost treasures of the Celts, once the most powerful grouping in Europe. There were certain rumors a century earlier: miners shrieked and blessed themselves when they found a Celt preserved in a salt-shaft, a victim of an avalanche. Even the contents of his stomach could help today's scientists to build up a picture of his life and times but we don't know where that salted fish of a man is anymore because the local priest pronounced him a devil and would not think of giving him a Christian burial. This conflict between *Christian* and *Celt* is central to the understanding of Ireland, tinting the literature, cosmology and folkways as it does with mystery and drama.

Is there a grain of truth behind Chesterton's amusing lines (or should we take them with a pinch of Hallstatt salt?):

The great Gaels of Ireland,
    The men whom God made mad,
    For all their wars are merry,
    And all their songs are sad.

Ancient commentators would nod vigorously, in approval. *Strabo,* a Greek geographer born around 64 B.C., stated, "The whole race … is madly fond of war." And the Greek historian, *Diodorus Siculus* (who features in a contemporary poem by Seamus Heaney) informs us that the Celts beheaded their enemies, attaching them to the necks of their horses. "They embalm in cedar oil the heads of the most distinguished enemies, and preserve them carefully in a chest, and display them with pride to strangers …"

Have things changed all that much? Not really! We still enjoy horse racing as much as we did 2,000 years ago: Epona, the horse deity, is the most widely represented goddess in the Celtic pantheon. Irish horses that race at the Cheltenham festival in England around and on St. Patrick's Day are referred to as "raiders," as are English horses that race at the Curragh, Punchestown or Fairyhouse. We've made a recovery since the English imposed Penal Laws, forbidding a Catholic to own a horse valued more than £5.00. We still enjoy gambling as we did 2,000 years ago: money lost on the horses at Cheltenham is often re-couped at cards in the early hours of the morning. *Diodorus*, were he alive today, might not temper or revise his descriptions of our drinking habits or our love of poetry.

The fate of the Celts in Europe was decided in *Alesia*, which in Celtic means "rocky hill." It was there that *Vercingétorix* withdrew from the Roman legions with 80,000 of his men. The legionnaires ringed the hill with fortifications, nine and a half miles in diameter. This was to keep the Gaulish Celts in and starve them to death. Now *Caesar* had to look to his back, fearing the arrival of a relief force. So he built another fortified ring—fourteen miles in diameter—and stocked up with provisions for his 40,000 men.

A quarter of a million Celts arrived, hoping to relieve *Vercingétorix* and his warriors. But the superiority of Roman tactics and cavalry won the day. *Vercingétorix* was put in chains and sent to Rome. Six years later he was paraded through the Forum. Then the Romans strangled him. His last gasp spelled the beginning of the decline of the Continental Celts. Gaulish Celtic became Latinized, eventually to become *French*.

There are three classes of men held in special honor: the *Bards*, the *Vates* and the *Druids*. The Bards are singers and poets; the Vates interpreters of sacrifice and natural philosophers; while the Druids in addition to the science of nature, study also moral philosophy … *Strabo*

## OGHAM

The earliest form of Irish is found on *Ogham* stones. *Ogma* (Gaulish *Ogmios*) was the Irish god who gave us the gift of writing. The alphabet was a unique one, whereby each marking denoted a tree. The 20 characters consisted of one or more straight lines carved, or drawn, perpendicularly—or at angle to a single long line, or to the edge of a stone or piece of wood. Thus **B** is *beith*, the birch—an infusion of its leaves was traditionally prized to add luster to the hair. **C** is *coll*, the hazel—the nuts produced a brew beloved of poets and seers. **D** is *dair*, the oak, found in many place names today, *Kildare* (Cill Dara), the oak church and *Derry* (Doire), meaning an oak grove. Oak groves were sacred to the druids and acorns were ceremoniously cut with silver sickles and collected in white sheets.

There are over 300 Ogham inscriptions and West Munster is a good place to view these standing stones. Some of them are pre-Christian, dating to the fourth century. After Ogham, we divide Irish into four main periods: *Old Irish* 600-900 A.D., *Middle Irish* 900-1200 A.D., *Classical Irish* 1200-1600 A.D., and *Modern Irish* 1600 until today. There is a wonderful innocence, a clear-eyed conciseness and a beguiling view of nature in Early Irish monastic lyrics:

> Jesukin!
> Child I nurse in my hut.
> What's the use in jewels a-plenty?
> All's illusion, save Jesukin.
> (St. Íde, died 572)
>
> ***
>
> Here's my news—
> the stag calls,
> summer over,
> winter squalls.
>
> Loud the cold wind,
> low the sun,
> brief its course,
> tides run.

Bracken red,
its shape not seen,
the wild goose raises
her familiar keen.

Frost congeals
the birds' wings,
time of ice,
these my tidings.
    (Ninth century, *trans*. G.R.)

"It was long thought that the rhyming, syllabic meters of Irish verse were formed under the influence of late Latin verse, but more recent scholarship argues just the opposite—that the versification of early Irish poetry influenced Medieval Latin verse. Certainly Latin verse in medieval Ireland would seem to reveal the impress of Celtic models in its technique; the most famous collection of poems in this style by the Irish Latinists is *Hisperica Famina* (seventh century). This hisperic or rhyming style was subsequently employed in the old English rhyming poem ..."

(*The Princeton Handbook of Multicultural Poetries*, Ed. T.V.F. Brogan, New Jersey, 1996.)

These early monastic lyrics forged a pietistic tradition which continue today. Many prayers and charms reveal a subtle, syncretic echo of Christian and pre-Christian values:

### Ortha Seirce agus Síorghrá

Ortha a chuir Muire in im,
Ortha seirce is síorghrá:
nár stada do cholainn
ach d'aire a bheith orm,
go leana do ghrá mo ghnaoi
mar leanas an bhó an lao
ón lá seo go lá mo bháis

### A Love Charm for Lasting Love

A charm the Virgin Mary put on the butter,
the love charm for lasting love:
may your body never cease
to pay me attention,
may your love follow my face
as the cow follows her calf
from this day until my last.

(From *Treasury of Irish Love Poems, Proverbs and Triads*, compiled and edited by Gabriel Rosenstock, Hippocrene Books, 1998.)

Celtic spirituality has found its own niche in the plethora of books available today on traditional wisdom. One such book, *Celtic Oracles*, by Rosemarie Anderson, Ph.D. (*Harmony Books*, New York, 1998) advertises itself as "a new system for spiritual growth and divination." Dr. Anderson intuits something about the Celtic past which is often ignored by those who examine linguistic or archaeological evidence in an overspecialized manner. She writes:

"Priestly authorities, such as druids, shamans, and healers, practiced ritual and alchemical healing and apprenticed younger men and women in their arts. Knowledge of medicine and herbs, law and ethical codes, and tribal traditions, as well as psychological and spiritual wisdom was recorded in vibrant and rhythmical verse. All of life—each season with its message, the flight of the birds at the hour of a child's birth, the spontaneous nuances to a well-known story—gave sacred semblance and direction to ordinary life events. If people were wise enough to read the signs, every moment was oracular, a prophecy amid the press of time ..."

As Ireland became Christianized, the poets continued to practice some of the functions of the ancient druids, just as pre-Christian gods and goddesses—notably Brigit—sacred wells and so on, took on the garb of Christianity. The word we have for a poet, *file*, means 'a seer'; one of our words for poetry, *éigse*, is cognate with *feiscint*, 'seeing'. The elaborate training of the apprentice poet, or bard, ensured that he would be a master of native lore, a king-maker. Thus the shamanistic role of the poet was never quite forgotten. Folklore attests to these powers and even Shakespeare refers to the rhyming powers of Irish bards to get rid of a plague of rats!

In all its vividness, its drama, its play of life, love, death, destiny and duty, this body of early work—a pre-Christian world view, possibly sanitized by monastic scribes—belongs to world literature. Some of the important early texts are the *Táin, The Voyage of Bran, The Madness of Sweeney, The Battle of Moytura, The Wooing of Etaín, Mac Con Glinne's Vision, The Story of Mac Dathó's Pig, Bricriu's Feast, The Colloquoy of the Ancients*. What epic films could be made on those two glorious cycles of hero tales, the Ulster Cycle (**Rúraíocht**) and the Fenian Cycle (**An Fhiannaíocht**), the great panorama of gods and men! The Fianna—Ireland's samurai—had more on their minds than the defense of the realm. Their human characteristics and failures are not looked over. Together they represent a handful of some of the greatest characters ever assembled in fiction.

It was this body of saga and poetry, as well as law texts, genealogies, historical tracts, "immrama" (mystical voyages), folklore and illuminated manuscripts that scholars and revolutionaries would turn to in the late nineteenth century, when it seemed that the Irish language was in irreversible decline, drawing inspiration from it towards the work at hand: cultural revival and nation-building.

## VIKINGS, NORMANS AND ENGLISH

A ninth century scribe wrote:

> Di thólu aechtrann et námat et geinte et fochide di phlágaibh tened et nóne et gorte et galrae n-ile n-écsamle …

> Save us from a flood of foreigners and foes and pagans and tribulations; from plagues of fire, famine and hunger and many diverse diseases…

Viking raiders came to Ireland looking for slaves and monastic plunder. Many poets and scholars fled the country. In a poem found in a monastery on the Continent, we read:

Is acher in gaíth innocht,
fu-fuasna fairggae findfholt ...

The wind tonight is fierce,
Tossing the sea's white hair ...

The poet goes on to say that in the safety of land-locked Switzerland, he needn't fear the fierce Vikings! Words originating from the Vikings give us an insight into the Scandinavian influence on Irish life:

**ancaire**, an anchor (*akkeri*)
**stiúir**, a rudder (*styri*)
**trosc**, a cod (*porskr*)
**scadán**, a herring (*skadd*)
**dorú**, a fishing line (*dorg*)
**margadh**, a market (*margad*)
**pingin**, a penny (*penningrs*)
**scilling**, a shilling (*skillingr*)
**cnaipe**, a button (*knappr*)
**bróg**, a shoe (*brók*)
**bogha**, a bow (*bogi*)
**builín**, a loaf of bread (*bylmingr*)
**beoir**, beer (*bjorr*)
**leag**, to knock down (*leggja*)
(Words borrowed from Welsh also exist such as **bainne** (milk) from *banne*.)

Assimilation occurred between the Vikings and the native Irish. The Viking name Ólàf was gaelicized as Amlaíb (Amhlaoibh) and three people of that name were kings of Dublin. One of them, Amhlaíb Cuarán, who died in 981, was a patron of poets and Cináed ua hArtacáin praised him thus:

Amhlaíb Átha Cliath cétaig
rogab rígi i mBeind Étair
tallus lúag mo dána de
ech d'echaib ána Aichle

Amhlaoibh of populous Dublin
Who ruled as King over Howth

I received the reward of my poem from him
A steed of the gracious steeds of Achall

The Viking invasions of the eighth century and the later Anglo-Norman invasions were periods of disruption and transition. The twelfth century reform of the church saw native learning pass into the charge of the Bardic Schools, keen to preserve what was left of the old order. The bards were employed by chieftains and composed *Duanairí* or anthologies of praise-poems, obituaries and the like. (In this brief sketch we cannot touch on the works of such bards as Eochaidh Ó hEoghusa and recommend a look at *The Oxford Companion to Irish Literature*, edited by Robert Welch, published by Oxford University Press, 1996.) The Norman influence on native poetry is seen in the courtly love poems or *amour courtois*.

The Statutes of Kilkenny (1366) sought to stem the Gaelicization of the Normans and in 1537 came *An Acte for the English Order, Habite and Language*. Among the words we owe to the Normans are the following: **aturnae**, attorney; **giúistís**, justice; **léas**, lease; **seirbhís**, service; **buidéal**, bottle; **cúirtéis**, courtesy.

The Gaelic order was about to crumble. The *Battle of Kinsale* (1601) and, later, *The Battle of the Boyne* (1690) were major defeats. The Flight of the Wild Geese, the native aristocracy, followed Kinsale. England was now in a position to flex its muscles, to take land in the form of "plantations" and impose penal laws, to "divide and conquer."

The Plantation of Ulster sowed the seeds of the bitter harvest of the latter half of the twentieth century. Even as it was happening, the Lord Chancellor, Sir Francis Bacon, writing in London, said, "Take it from me that the bane of a plantation is when the undertakers or planters make such haste to a little mechanical present profit, as disturbeth the whole frame and nobleness of the work for times to come . . ."

The Cromwellian settlements of 1652-54 appropriated 11 million acres. The cry was, "To Hell or to Connaught."

A poetry of vitriol, chagrin and false hope emerged in the work of **Dáibhí Ó Bruadair** (1625-98) and **Aogán Ó Rathaille**. (Readers of English should refer to translations of these poets by Michael Hartnett.) Ó Rathaille (1675-1729) is remembered for his *aisling* or vision-poetry, composed in Jacobite times, when Ireland appears to him as a woman, mourning the state of the nation.

There was no place for Irish in the new English order. Daniel O'Connell, known as "The Liberator," champion of Catholic Emancipation, himself a native Irish speaker, wrote to a friend in this manner: "Therefore, although the Irish language is connected with many recollections that twine around the hearts of Irishmen, yet the superior utility of the English tongue, as the medium of all modern communication, is so great that I can witness without a sigh the gradual disuse of Irish ..." O'Connell's aunt was Eibhlín Dubh Ní Chonaill. Was her great *Lament for Art O'Leary* also a lament for a world that would never be again?

**Mo chara thu go daingean**
**Is níor chreideas riamh dod mharbh ...**

My love forever!
I never thought of you dead
Till your horse came home
Trailing her reins
And your heartsblood smeared
From her face to tooled saddle
Where you used to sit and stand.
I gave one jump to the threshold
The next to the gate
The third astride your horse.
I clapped my hands
And galloped off
As fast as was in me
Till I found you dead
Beside a little furze bush
Without a pope or a bishop
Cleric or priest
Who might read a psalm for you
But a tired old woman
Who spread her cloak upon you—
As your blood gushed forth

I did not stop to wipe it
But drank it up in handfuls ...
> (Trans. Seán Mac Mathúna, *Treasury of Irish Love Poems,*
> *Proverbs & Triads*, Hippocrene Books, pp. 40-51.)

**Maynooth**, a seminary for priests, accepted the growth of anglicization and clergy were soon putting a stop to "pagan" practices, such as the wake, and dancing at crossroads. **The Great Famine** of the mid-nineteenth century brought death and misery in calamitous proportions and emigration became endemic. The "superior utility of the English tongue," as the "Liberator" had it, began to sound truer every day, so that Irish-speaking parents agreed to a "tally stick" being placed around their children's necks. The stick was notched every time they were caught speaking Irish and punishment exacted according to these Ogham-like notches! Scholars, many of them German and Scandinavian, began to take an interest in the language and native societies sprang up of an academic or antiquarian nature. Then came a note of hope with the foundation of Conradh na Gaeilge, The Gaelic League, whose founders **Douglas Hyde** and **Eoin Mac Néill** looked to a social and cultural revival that might reverse the tide of anglicization. The League was part of the ferment that lead to the **Rising**, in **Easter 1916**, seeking separation from Britain and Irish cultural autonomy.

Did all this come too late? Though many towns and cities had become anglicized since the Middle Ages, there were at least 3 million Irish speakers in pre-Famine days. The number of native speakers today is probably less than 30,000 ...

Census figures, so far, reflect wishful thinking rather than actual patterns of daily usage. The 1996 census would lead us to believe that 43% of the population, i.e. 1.4 million can speak Irish, but two thirds of this 1.4 million do not use it, or use it less frequently than once a week. I once asked a farmer in North Kerry if there was any Irish in the area, or did he himself have any knowledge of it. *"Th'anam 'on diabhal,* not a *siolla!"* he responded, stoutly—"your soul to the devil, not a syllable," was his reply, in English, or so he thought! I had come too late! Daniel O'Connell had got to him before me.

With concerted language planning—especially in Gaeltacht[1] areas—and with more innovative use of materials in schools, the language should be around in 200 years time. It is impossible to look any further than that, except to a cultural revolution that might finish off the business begun by the Gaelic League ... the globalization of culture, still in its incipient stage, may be a catalyst for that event.

"How curiously might one speculate if one were to imagine that when the delvers of the fifteenth century unearthed the buried literatures of Greece and Rome they had stumbled instead upon that other buried literature which was to remain in the dust of the libraries for four centuries longer! Then instead of the classical revival we should have the Celtic revival; or rather the Celtic would have become the classic and the Gael would have given laws to Europe. I do not say positively that literature would have gained, but I am not sure that it would have lost. Something it would have lost: the Greek ideal of perfection in form, the wise calm Greek scrutiny. Yet something it would have gained: a more piercing vision, a nobler, because a more human, inspiration, above all a deeper spirituality ..." *Patrick H. Pearse*

## IRISH DIALECTS

In the sixteenth century there was little difference between **Irish** and **Scots Gaelic**. There are many differences today between the two languages and, also, between the three main dialects of Irish—**Ulster**, **Connaught** and **Munster**.

**English:** How are you, Mary?
**Gaelic:** Ciamar a tha sibh, a Mhàiri?
**Ulster:** Cad é mar tá tú, a Mháire?
**Connaught:** Cén chaoi a bhfuil tú, a Mháire?
**Munster:** Conas tá tú, a Mháire?

---

1. A *Gaeltacht* is an area in which Irish is the main medium of communication, especially among the older generation. A *Breac-Ghaeltacht* describes an area in which both languages are generally used.

It is usual for somebody who progresses from *Beginner's Irish* to con-
centrate on one particular dialect and to become familiar with the literature, idioms and songs of that dialect. But if you have a good ear, you
should try to have at least passive knowledge of the three major dialects.
If you hear the emphasis on the second syllable in *misneach* (courage)
you are listening to a speaker of Munster Irish (**Kerry**, **Cork**, **Waterford**).

## FURTHER READING AND STUDY

### Irish Language and Literature
Ball, M.J., ed. *The Celtic Languages*. London, 1993.
De Blacam, Aodh. *Gaelic Literature Surveyed*. Dublin, 1929; re-issued
    1973.
De Fréine, Seán. *The Great Silence*. Dublin, 1965.
Fitzmaurice, Gabriel and Kiberd, Declan, eds. *An Crann faoi Bhláth/
    The Flowering Tree*. Dublin, 1995.
Greene, David. *The Irish Language*. Dublin, 1966.
Hindley, Reg. *The Death of the Irish Language*. London, 1990.
Lee, J.J. *Ireland 1912-1985: Politics and Society*. Cambridge, 1989.
Lehmann, R.P.M. and W.P. *An Introduction to Old Irish*. New York, 1975.
Mac Cana, Proinsias. *Literature in Irish*. Dublin, 1980.
Mac Póilín, Aodán, ed. *The Irish Language in Northern Ireland*.
    Belfast, 1997.
Mc Mahon, Sean and O'Donoghue, Jo, eds. *The Mercier Companion to
    Irish Literature*. Cork & Dublin, 1998.
Ó Cuív, Brian, ed. *A View of the Irish Language*. Dublin, 1969.
Ó Fearaíl, Pádraig. *The Story of Conradh na Gaeilge*. Dublin, 1975.
Ó Murchú, Máirtín. *The Irish Language*. Dublin, 1985.
Ó Tuama, Seán and Kinsella, Thomas, eds. *An Duanaire 1600-1900:
    Poems of the Dispossessed*. Dublin, 1981.
Ó Tuama, Seán, ed. *The Gaelic League Idea*. Cork, 1972.
Purdon, Edward. *The Story of the Irish Language*. Cork & Dublin, 1999.
    *Report of the Committee on Irish Language Attitudes Research*.
    Dublin, 1981.
Rosenstock, Gabriel, ed. *A Treasury of Irish Love Poems, Proverbs and
    Triads*. New York, 1998.
Welch, Robert, ed. *The Oxford Companion to Irish Literature*. Oxford,
    1996.

## Language Instruction

*An Dréimire* and *An Staighre*. Dublin, Anois Teo., 27 Cearnóg Mhurfean, Baile Átha Cliath. (Authentic reading material for learners, with cassette.)

An Roinn Oideachais (Department of Education). *Foclóir Póca: English-Irish/Irish-English Dictionary*. Dublin, An Gúm, 1986. (Pocket dictionary; the first Irish dictionary to include a pronunciation guide in phonetic script for each headword.)

An Roinn Oideachais (Department of Education). *Foclóir Scoile*. Dublin, An Gúm, 1994. (A revised version of the *Foclóir Póca*. Contains some additional terms provided by the Department's Terminology Committee.)

Bammesberger, Alfred. *A Handbook of Irish. 1. Essentials of Modern Irish. 2. An Outline of Modern Irish Grammar*. Heidelberg, 1982 & 1983.

De Bhaldraithe, Tomás, ed. *English-Irish Dictionary*. Dublin, 1959.

Linguaphone Institute/Gael-Linn. *Cúrsa Gaeilge (Irish Course and Irish Course Handbook)*. London, Linguaphone Institute; Dublin, Gael-Linn, 1974. (2 books & 8 cassettes.)

McGonagle, Noel. *Irish Grammar: A Basic Handbook*. Galway, 1988. (Designed for learners who wish to avoid the more complex points of Irish grammar.)

Ó Baoill, Dónall P., ed. *Foclóir póca - Learner's Cassette*. Dublin, 1986. (Produced to accompany An Gúm's *Foclóir Póca: [Pocket] English-Irish/Irish-English Dictionary*.)

Ó Baoill, Dónall P. *Cleachtaí foghraíochta*. Dublin, 1989. (Booklet and accompanying tapes—Ulster, Connacht or Munster Irish.)

Ó Dónaill, Éamonn and Ní Churraighín, Deirbhile. *Now You're Talking: A Multimedia Course for Beginners*. Dublin, 1995. (A course based on the RTÉ/BBC Northern Ireland television course. Designed for complete beginners and those wishing to brush up their Irish. Course book & three audio cassettes.)

Ó Dónaill, Éamonn and Ní Mhaonaigh, Siuán. *Abair leat! Cúrsa ranga do mhúinteoirí daoine fásta, leibhéal 1, cuid 1*. Béal Feirste (Belfast), Iontaobhas Ultach, i gcomhar le hÚdarás na Gaeltachta, 1996. (A practical course for *teachers* of Irish to adult beginners. While Ulster Irish is used throughout, other dialects can be taught as required. Practical advice is given on how to plan the lessons and teach Irish effectively. Cassettes and materials which can be photocopied for class use are provided instead of course books.)

Ó Dónaill, Niall. *Foclóir Gaeilge/Béarla*. Dublin, 1977. (The standard Irish-English dictionary.)

Ó Sé, Diarmuid and Sheils, Joe. *Teach Yourself Irish: a Complete Course for Beginners*. Revised edition. London, 1993. (Book & cassette.)

Ó Siadhail, Mícheál. *Learning Irish: An Introductory Self-tutor*. Dublin Institute for Advanced Studies, 1980.
German edition: *Lehrbuch der irischen Sprache*. Edited by Arndt Wigger. Hamburg, Helmut Buske, 1985. (Book & cassettes. English language edition also available from Yale University Press. Book & 3 cassettes. Based on the dialect of Cois Fharraige, County Galway.)

The Christian Brothers. *Graiméar Gaeilge na mBráithre Críostaí*. Dublin, An Gúm, 1999.

All these titles should be available from **ÁIS**, a book distribution agency. Over 100 books are published annually in Irish. For information, contact:

ÁIS, 31 Sráid na bhFíníní, Baile Átha Cliath 2, Ireland.

Please note that orders are accepted only from booksellers and libraries.

In the United States, contact:

**The Irish Bookstore**, 580 Broadway, Room 1103, New York, NY 10012. Tel: (212) 274-1923.

# Irish Names

Place names, street names, surnames and Christian (or pre-Christian) names can give us an insight into Ireland and the Irish language. Let us start, therefore, with Ireland itself.

**Seathrún Céitinn** (Geoffrey Keating, 1570-1650) in his *Foras Feasa ar Éirinn*, of which hundreds of manuscript copies were made—one by poet **Aogán Ó Rathaille** housed in the National Library of Ireland—gives us 14 of the countless number of names given to Ireland, commencing with **Inis na bhFíobhadh**, the island of woods. It is said that Ireland was once so covered in woods that a squirrel could traverse the country, from north to south, without setting foot on the ground. The second name was **Críoch na bhFuiníoch** meaning the world's end—*fuin* being related to Latin *finis*. The third name was **Inis Ealga**; *inis* means "island" and *ealga* denotes "noble." Many island names are preceded by *inis*, or use *inis* as a suffix, such as **Inis Arcáin**, Sherkin Island, County Cork; **Inis Bó Finne**, Inishbofin (literally the island of the fair cow) off County Donegal and an island of the same name off County Galway; **Inis Oírr**, Inisheer, the smallest of the Aran islands, predominantly Irish-speaking, **Inis Mac Neasáin**, Ireland's Eye, County Dublin—"eye" in this case is "øy" Old Norse for "island," and so on.

Three common names for Ireland, beloved of poets, are **Éire** (Éiriú), **Banba** and **Fódla**—the fourth, fifth and sixth names, respectively: these were goddesses or queens of the magical race of **Tuatha Dé Danann**.

The seventh name was **Inis Fáil**. The **Lia Fáil** was the phallic stone of Tara, the Stone of Destiny, which shrieked at the inauguration of the rightful High King of Ireland.

The eighth name was **Muicinis**, Pig Island. **Scotia** was the ninth name. *Scotus*, in olden times, meant Irish, not Scottish, and there was an eminent philosopher known as Scotus. **Hibernia** the tenth, **Iernia** the eleventh, **Irin** the twelfth, **Irlanda** the thirteenth (after **Ír**, the first man to be buried in Ireland, according to lore) and the fourteenth name **Ogigia**, signified the "isle of antiquity." And there are another 200 names, at least.


## SURNAMES

Ireland was one of the first countries to introduce hereditary surnames, over a thousand years ago. There are more **Ó** (**O'**) names than **Mac** (Mc) names in Ireland. *Mac* is a "son" and *ó* is a "grandson." They began to go out of use in the seventeenth and eighteenth century and their revival was encouraged by the Gaelic League.

It is extremely common to hear death notices on the Irish language radio stations, **Raidió na Gaeltachta** and **Raidió na Life**, giving two or possibly three different versions of a name. So, if a John Ward died, we would hear that name, the Irish version, Seán Mac an Bhaird (meaning "son of the bard") and possibly the name he was best known by, Seáinín Chití (*ín* an affectionate diminutive, and the name of his mother, Kitty, or the name of his father, or a place name, or name associated with a trade or profession attached to his name).

An agnomen is a name added to a family name. Thus, **Seán Ó Tuama an Ghrinn** (1708-1775), a poet and innkeeper. **Greann:** merriment; genitive case **grinn**, aspirated after the definite article, **an**, to mean **Seán Ó Tuama of the Merriment**.

Nicknames include **láidir**, strong, as in **Tomás Láidir Ó Coisteala**, a seventeenth century poet; **rua** (red-haired) or **dall** (blind), as in the poet **Séamas Dall Mac Cuarta** (1650-1733), or **bán** (fair-haired), as in **Tomás Bán Ó Coincheanainn** (1870-1961), an Aran-born Gaelic Leaguer, or **beag** (small), as in County Louth poet, **Peadar Beag Ó Doirnín** (1702-1769) or **óg** (young), **Tadhg Óg Ó hUiginn**, a fifteenth century Galway poet. **Ó hUiginn**, by the way, is anglicized as **Higgins** but if you look at the Irish **Uiginn**, you can clearly see by substituting the **U** with a **V** and the **g** with a **k**, that you have a Viking …

Edward MacLysaght, an authority on Irish family names, recalled in his diary how he came across many bizarre surnames in post-seventeenth century Ireland, such as **Bogus, Brothel, Horror, Jealous, Rotten, Farty, Sex, Rape, Twaddle** etc. Many of these idiotic names were, in fact, bastardizations of fine old Irish names, anglicized to ridiculousness. *Farty* would be **Ó Fathartaigh**, for instance.

**Dubhghlas de híde** (Douglas Hyde, 1860-1949), co-founder of the Gaelic League and first President of Ireland, once inquired about the surname Rabbit. An informant told him that it was quite common in County Galway.
"I'm a rabbit myself."
"That's not an Irish name," said I.
"Thrue for ye; me rale name is Ó Coinín, which is Rabbit when Englished ..."

## SOME IRISH NAMES FOR GIRLS

**Áine**—delightful, brilliant. Anglicized as *Anne*.
**Aisling**—a vision. Anglicized as *Ashling*.
**Aoife**—radiant, pleasant, beautiful.
**Béibhinn**—fair lady.
**Bláithín**—little flower. (The sobriquet on the Blasket Island of the English scholar, Robin Flower, mentor to Tomás Ó Criomhthain, author of **An tOileánach** / *The Islandman*).
**Bóinn**—cow-white, goddess of the Boyne. Rarely used as a name but worthy of revival!
**Bríd**—exalted one, high goddess. The feast of the Christian saint who substituted for the goddess falls on February 1ST, the beginning of Spring in Ireland.
**Clíodhna**—We are informed by Dr. Daithí Ó hÓgáin in his *Myth, Legend and Romance, An Encyclopaedia of the Irish Folk Tradition* (Ryan, 1990):
A medieval story tells of how she fell in love with Aonghus and went from her dwelling in Magh Meall ("the pleasant plain") in a bronze boat to meet him. She was accompanied by a man called Iuchna, who acted treacherously towards her. He played magic music so that she fell asleep, and a great flood came and drowned her at Cuan Dor

(the bay of Glandore, County Cork). An alternative account makes her one of the Tuatha Dé Danann, and states that she eloped from Tír Tairngire ("the Land of Promise") with a handsome young warrior called Ciabhán. They landed at Trá Théite (the strand at Glandore) and Ciabhán left her in his boat while he went to hunt. The wave then came and drowned her. These accounts seem to have arisen from an actual designation of the tide at that place as the Wave ("Tonn") of Clíona. This was one of the great waves of Ireland, according to the ancient topographical system, and her association with it was an expression of the idea that the deities resided in water ...

**Cneas**—literally "skin"; by association, fair, beautiful. The genitive is *cnis* as in *cara cnis* bosom friend and *éadach cnis*, underwear.

**Dar Óma**—daughter of the god Ogma. (See section on *Ogham*, page 5.)

**Deirdre**—the tragic heroine of the great Ulster Cycle of heroic tales, *an Rúraíocht*.

**Éadaoin**—see poem *Lovely Lady* in *A Treasury of Irish Love* (Hippocrene Books, 1998).

**Eithne**—kernel of a nut. She grew up in Brugh na Bóinne (Newgrange), her diet for many years consisting of the milk of two cows from India.

**Émer**—chosen by the warrior, Cú Chulainn, for her six gifts: charm, singing, sweet-sounding speech, needlework, wisdom, and purity.

**Féthnat**—a musician to the Tuatha Dé Danann.

**Fionnuala**—from "fionn" meaning "fair"—a name in itself and a popular prefix—and "guala" meaning "a shoulder." A daughter of Lear Shí Fionnachaidh of the *Clann Lir* tale of woe. She and her brothers, Aodh, Conn and Fiachra, were transformed into swans for nine hundred years until the spell was broken by St. Mochaomhóg.

**Geiléis**  from "geal" (bright) and "géis" (swan).

**Gráinne**—a grain-goddess, from "grán" (grain), in all probability. *The Pursuit of Diarmaid and Gráinne* is one of the most enduring love stories of world literature and the name *Diarmaid* is derived from *dífhormaid*, "without envy."

**Grian**—sun-goddess. There are many beautiful names associated with light—**Niamh** (luster), **Lasair** (flame), **Lasairíona** (flame of wine) and the name of the god **Lugh** (as in the festival of Lughnasa) means "light."

**Liadhain**—see first and last poem in *A Treasury of Irish Love* (Hippocrene Books, 1998).

**Macha**—see note to poem of that name in *A Treasury of Irish Love*.

**Méabh**—intoxicating.

**Mis**—she drank the blood from her dead father's wounds and went crazy. She regained her senses when Dubh Rois, the king's harper, played music for her, bathed her and taught her culinary skills. She had been eating animal and human flesh up until then. See Biddy Jenkinson's poem in *A Treasury of Irish Love*.

**Mór**—great. Many streams owe their origin, in folklore, to her prodigious urination. *Mór dhuit* (or *Mora dhuit*) is a common greeting, especially in Munster. The reply is, *Mór is Muire duit*, "Mór and Mary to you." An expression to denote the transitoriness of all phenomena is *leá mhún Mhóire*, "the evaporation of Mór's urine."

**Muireann**—*muir*, "the sea" and *fionn*, "fair"—as bright as the waves of the sea.

**Órla**—*ór*, "gold" and *flaith* "princess/prince."

**Osnait**—a little deer.


## SOME NAMES FOR BOYS

**Ainle**—hero. He, Naoise and Ardán are Clann Uisnigh, the sons of Uisneach, famed in legend.

**Amhairghin**—born of song. The poet-druid **Amhairghin Glúngheal** ("Bright-Kneed") reputedly recited the first poem heard in Ireland, the mysterious *Am gaeth ar muir*, "I am the Wind on the Sea ..." which is Vedic-like in cosmic consciousness.

**Aodh**—fire. Anglicized as Hugh. Root of surnames **Hayes, Mc Hugh, Mc Coy**, etc. Diminutive: **Aodhán** or **Aogán**.

**Aonghus**—Son of the Daghda. Many poets of the Ó Dálaigh sept bear this name: **Aonghus Mac Daighre Ó Dálaigh** (1540-1601), **Aonghus Fionn Ó Dálaigh** (1520-1570) and **Aonghus na nAor Ó Dálaigh** (died 1617) who was employed by Lord Mountjoy and Lord Carew to satirize the native Gaels.

**Art**—a bear, a champion. **Art Mac Cumhaigh** (1715-1773) was an Ulster poet, still fondly remembered today.

**Bardán**—a poet, or bard.

**Beag**—small. **Beag Mac Dé** (son of God) was a prophet who died in 533 A.D. When he was born people remarked how tiny he was, whereupon Beag spoke up and said he was, indeed, small but he had no small knowledge of matters esoteric and exoteric. He once spoke to nine people simultaneously; if you can imagine such a feat.

**Beoán**—lively fellow. On a mission to Rome he was distracted by a mermaid by name of Lí Ban.

**Blámhac**—renowned son. Name of a great eighth century poet.

**Bran**—a raven. The name of one of Fionn Mac Cumhail's hunting hounds ... feeling the brunt of his master's anger, poor Bran went off and drowned himself.

**Breandán/Bréanainn**—anglicized as **Brendan**. Sixth century Kerry saint who may have "discovered" America. The *Navigatio Brendani* was a medieval bestseller throughout Europe. Remembered on May 16 when pilgrims climb Mount Brandon.

**Brian**—famous Brians include **Brian Boru** (926-1014 A.D.), High King of Ireland and **Brian Merriman** (1749-1805), author of the long, rabelaisian poem, *Cúirt an Mheoin Oíche* (The Midnight Court).

**Bricriu**—The satirist featured in the ninth century text *Scéla Muice Meic Dathó* (The Story of the Pig of Mac Dá Thó) in which the Ulster hero, Conall Cearnach, says: "I swear to you as my people swear that since the very first day I held a spear, there's not a day I haven't slain a Connaughtman ..." Such interprovincial rivalries are still common today, especially in the sphere of hurling and Gaelic football.

**Buach**—victorious.

**Cairbre**—apart from being the name of many rulers and many saints, it was also the name of a lion in the Dublin Zoo that roared at the commencement of films. Root of surname **Carberry**—a father, trainer, and son, jockey, of that name won the 1999 English Grand National.

**Caoilte**—one of the Fianna band of warriors.

**Caoimhín**—beautiful birth. Anglicized as **Kevin**. Founder of the sixth century monastic settlement in Glendalough (**Gleann Dá Loch**), Glen of the two Lakes. His self-mortification knew no bounds and he once did a seven-year stint eating nothing but nettles and sorrel. While he was in a meditative pose, a blackbird made her nest on his outstretched hands. Caoimhín remained in this pose until her eggs were hatched.

**Caolán**—slender lad.

**Caomhán**—beloved.

**Cathal**—strong in battle. Anglicized as **Charles**. Name of a King of Connaught, Cathal Crobhdhearg ("of the wine-red hand"). First name of such poets as **Cathal Buí Mac Giolla Ghunna** (1690-1756), author of *An Bonnán Buí* (The Yellow Bittern) and contemporary Donegal poet, **Cathal Ó Searcaigh**.

**Ciarán**—founder of Clonmacnoise monastery in the sixth century. During his student days a stag would oblige him by holding a book in its antlers until he had finished studying.

**Colm**—a dove. Colm Cille ("dove of the church"), along with Bríd and Pádraig, one of the three great thaumaturges of Ireland. In 546 he founded a monastery, Doire Cholm Cille. (*Doire* is an oak grove, anglicized *Derry* and called *Londonderry* by colonists.)

**Comhdhán**—seventh century jester, driven daft by a cuckolded druid.

**Cormac**—name of several rulers and saints.

**Cuán**—diminutive of Cú, hound.

**Cuirithir**—see first and last poem in *A Treasury of Irish Love* (Hippocrene Books, 1998).

**Eolang**—confessor to Barra, patron saint of Cork. But since it has been proven that Barra never existed, maybe Eolang is also a figment.

**Feardorcha**—dark man. Anglicized as **Frederick**.

**Féichín**—little raven (diminutive of Fiach). Seventh century founder of a monastery in County Westmeath.

**Find**—ancient personification of wisdom.

**Fionn**—fair. Irish hero, Celtic avatar. Wien (Vienna) owe its name to him.

**Fionnchú**—fair-haired hound/hero. Seventh century saint, skilled in the arts of selfmortification.

**Fursa**—seventh century monk, much bothered by devils and visions. One of his visions was the talk of Europe at one stage and is said to have influenced Dante's *Divine Comedy*.

**Gael**—Irishman. Gael Glas, grandson of Míl, was said to have invented the Irish language from the 72 languages then spoken.

**Guaire**—King of Connaught, the most generous man of the seventh century. He just couldn't stop giving—even after his death! As his body was being brought to Clonmacnoise for burial, the dead Guaire stretched out his hand, throwing a fistful of sand at a beggar. The sand turned to grains of gold.

**Labhradh**—speaker. The story of King Labhradh of the Horse-Ears is known to many Irish school children.

**Leannán**—lover.

**Mac Dara**—son of the oak.

**Manannán**—rarely used today, but deserving of a revival. The name relates to the Isle of Man. Manannán Mac Lir (*lear* = sea, *mac* = son; son of the sea) is the sea god, a Celtic Poseidon.

Many families keep the same Christian names from one generation to the next. **Peadar Ó Laoghaire** (1839-1920) tells us in his autobiography, *Mo Scéal Féin*, that Conchúr, Art, Fear, etc. were personal names associated with his people. When a married couple lost one child after another, a mysterious woman came all the way from Kildare to County Cork to say that the next child would live if given an "ainm cúl le cine," a foreign name not associated with the family. The boy was named Barnabí—and he lived.

**Maol Íosa**—devotee of Jesus. The eleventh century Donegal poet **Maol Íosa Ó Brolachán** wrote a poem asking the Lord to protect him and all his parts, including his belly that he might not eat too much.

**Maoleachlainn**—Anglicized as **Malachy**. In 1139 a saint by this name set out for Rome and when he neared his destination fell to the ground and muttered cryptic verses in Latin. Buried for centuries in the Vatican, the prophecies surrounding various popes tell us that only two popes remain after Pope John Paul II. (He has been 90% right up to now ...)

**Maon**—silent. Name of a largely forgotten god.

**Mír**—Son of the Daghda (Good God), lover of Éadaoin. See *Lovely Lady* in *A Treasury of Irish Love*, (Hippocrene Books, 1998).

**Mochaoi**—sixth century abbot who went AWOL. He was collecting timber to build a church and while in the forest he stopped to listen to a bird. The bird warbled three times. When Mochaoi returned he found an oratory had been built to his memory! (Each warble lasted 50 years.)

**Mochuda**—beloved. An abbot of this name was said to be the handsomest man of the seventh century.

**Moling**—holy leaper. Eighth century saint, still honored in County Carlow, who had a pet fly of unusual musical ability.

**Molua**—sixth century saint who could light a candle with his breath.

**Murchú**—hound of the sea. Anglicized as **Murphy**.

**Nuadha**—cloud maker.

**Oisín**—little deer. Son of Fionn.

**Oscar**—deer lover.

**Pádraig**—Anglicized as **Patrick, Paddy, Paud**. All p-words in Irish come from Latin, such as *póg*, a kiss (from *pax*, peace, as in "the kiss of peace").

**Rónán**—little seal.

**Ruairí**—great king. Anglicized as **Rory**.

**Rumann**—**Rumann Mac Colmáin**, eighth century poet, commissioned by the Vikings to compose a poem in praise of the sea. "As to my fee," said Rumann, "one penny from every bad Viking and two pennies from every good Viking." They all coughed up tuppence!

**Seanchán**—man of lore. Seventh century poet, said to have discovered the lost epic of the *The Táin*.

**Suibhne**—anglicized as **Sweeney**. The sequence of poems by **Suibhne Geilt**, Mad Sweeney, who took to the trees like a bird, belongs to world literature: *Duairc in betha beith gan tech ...* "Gloomy the life without a house; a wretched life, gentle Christ: nothing for food but green cress, nothing but clear stream-water to drink ..."

**Tadhg**—Eccentric lexicographer Dinneen says of this name, sometimes anglicized as Thady: "the typical Irishman, especially the plebian type, while Diarmaid seems applicable to the upper class." Protestants in Northern Ireland sometimes refer to a Catholic as a **Taigue**.

**Ultán**—an Ulsterman.

**Urard**—One **Urard Mac Coise** was a poet, scholar and miracle worker who died in Clonmacnoise in the year 990.


## FURTHER READING

*Gazetteer of Ireland*. Dublin, 1989. (Prepared by the Placenames Branch of the Ordnance Survey of the Irish Government.)

Mac Lysaght, Edward. *Irish Families: Their Names, Arms and Origins*. Dublin, 1985.

Mac Lysaght, Edward. *The Surnames of Ireland*. Dublin, 1997.

Ó Corráin, Donnchadha and Maguire, Fidelma. *Gaelic Personal Names*. Dublin, 1981.

Todd, Loreto. *Celtic Names for Children*. Boulder, 1998.

# Geography and Tourism

There are *Gaeltacht* areas in **County Donegal**, including Tory Island; in **County Galway**—Connemara and the Aran Islands; and in **County Kerry**—the Dingle Peninsula. There are smaller *Gaeltachtaí* in **County Cork, County Waterford, County Mayo** and **County Meath**.

The *Gaeltacht* areas of the west of Ireland contain some of the most ruggedly beautiful scenery in Ireland.

*GaelSaoire* is a new initiative in cultural tourism and can be contacted at Údarás na Gaeltachta, Na Forbacha, Galway.
Website: http://www.udaras.ie

The *Údarás* is the *Gaeltacht* authority which runs development programs in the fields of industry, fisheries, communications, traditional skills, education and tourism.

## IRISH MEDIA

There are about 30,000 native speakers of Irish who use Irish on a daily basis and about 100,000 non-native speakers. The rest of the population would have rusty "school Irish."

There are two weekly newspapers in Irish, *LÁ*, published in Belfast (www.nuacht.com) and *Foinse* published in Connemara. The main monthly magazines are *Comhar, Cuisle, Feasta* and *An tUltach*. Back issues of the literary journals *Scríobh, Innti* and *Oghma* are indicators of the vitality of modern Irish writing. *An Léitheoir* is a quarterly bilingual newsletter giving information on new books from Irish-language publishers, such as An Gúm, Cló Iar-Chonnachta, Coiscéim, An Clóchomhar and Sáirséal Ó Marcaigh. *An Léitheoir* is distributed free with the journal *Books Ireland*.

Irish speakers are served by **Raidió na Gaeltachta** which was founded in 1972. It has studios in Casla (**Connemara**), Na Doirí Beaga (**Donegal**), Baile na nGall (**Kerry**), Castlebar (**Mayo**) and **Dublin**. Its archives have been transferred to CD-ROM and will be an invaluable resource for future students of the language.

For details of satellite broadcasting programs by Raidió na Gaeltachta, see www.rnag.ie.

**Teilifís na Gaeilge** (now called TG4) was established in 1996 and has given a shot in the arm to independent TV companies. Its success has confounded the sceptics, especially the anti-Irish sections of the media. Website: http://www.tg4.ie

## FESTIVALS

If you are planning a visit to a Gaeltacht area, make it coincide with a festival if possible. Here are some pointers, starting with **Connemara** and **Clare**.

*Early April* (c. 1-3): *Féile Joe Einniú*, in **Carna**, in memory of the great *sean-nós* singer, Joe Heaney.

*Early April* (c. 8-10): *Siamsa Choilm de Bhailís*, in **Leitir Móir**, in memory of the poet who died in the Poorhouse.

*Mid-June* (c. 13-14): *Féile na gCurachaí* in **An Spidéal**. Curragh racing.

*End-June* (c. 26-28): *An Patrún* in **Inis Mór, Aran**.

*Early July* (c. 4-12): *Scoil Shamraidh Willie Clancy*, in **Miltown Malbay**, County Clare. Not a Gaeltacht area, but this festival in memory of the legendary piper is, along with the *The Merriman School* (no fixed abode), one of the cultural highlights of the summer.

*Early August* (c. 7-9): *Cruinniú na mBád*, Kinvara, County Clare. For those who love boats: turf boats and other traditional craft.

*Mid-September* (c. 16-20): *Pléaráca Chonamara*, in Connemara. Music and mayhem!

Next we look at **Donegal**:

*Late April* (c. 27- ): *Éigse Uladh* in **Gaoth Dobhair** (Gweedore).

*Early June* (12 -): *Féile Seiteanna* in Oileán Thoraigh (Tory Island).

Set-dancing on an island famous for its primitive painters, one of
whom is the king of the island.
*Late December: Scoil Gheimhridh Frankie Kennedy* in Gaoth Dobhair.
The cream of Irish music and master classes.

And now to **Munster**:
*Feast of St. Brigid* (1st Feb.): *Éigse na Brídeoige* in Ballinskelligs area
of South Kerry.
*Early May* (May Day): *Féile na Bealtaine* in **An Daingean** (Dingle). Lit-
erary events, carousing and lots of coffee the following morning in
An Caifé Liteartha (bookshop cum café). The Blasket Heritage
Centre is well worth a visit.
*Mid-April* (c. 14-19): *Féile Phan Cheilteach* in Tralee, County Kerry.
Pan-Celtic shenanigans.

For an update on these and other festivals contact: An Rannóg For-
bartha Teanga agus Cultúir, **Údarás na Gaeltachta**, Na Forbacha,
Gaillimh, Ireland. e-mail: eolas@udaras.ie

*Éigsí:* weekend cultural festivals, called *Éigsí,* are organized in various
localities around Ireland. Information: **Comhdháil Náisiúnta na Gaeilge**,
46 Kildare St., Dublin, Ireland. Visit their restaurant downstairs!

*An tOireachtas* is an annual gathering of Gaels, the highlight of
which is the *sean-nós* (unaccompanied old-style singing) competitions.
It is run by Conradh na Gaeilge/The Gaelic League: 6 Harcourt St.,
Dublin 2, Ireland.

### IRISH LANGUAGE EDUCATION—
### LEARNING IRISH IN THE GAELTACHT

The most natural way to learn a language is among native speakers.
This can be achieved by attending an adult language course in the
Gaeltacht. It could prove to be one of the most enjoyable holidays of
your life.

First decide which dialect you wish to master, Ulster, Connaught or
Munster. If you pick *Ulster*, then your destination is magical Donegal.
**Oideas Gael** is situated in Glencolumbkille, close to the Gaeltacht ...
the murmur of bees, the bleating of sheep, whispering waves ... Gleann

Cholm Cille offers a magic potion. Here the teaching of Irish is a memorable and fun experience, with a host of extra-curricular activities such as tapestry and hill-walking. Further information from: Liam Ó Cuinneagáin, **Oideas Gael**, Gleann Cholm Cille, Contae Dhún na nGall, Ireland.

Another Donegal-based course is in **Gweedore** where you can acquire skills in conversational Irish. Details from An Chrannóg, Na Doirí Beaga, Leitir Ceanainn, Contae Dhún na nGall, Ireland.

Or you may wish to spend more time in Dublin, to enjoy the theaters, pubs and restaurants. If so, find out about basic conversation classes from **Gael-Linn**, 26 Merrion Square, Dublin 2. (You may also be interested in their excellent CD catalog of Irish Music.)

If *Connaught* Irish is your choice, you will be in good hands in **Áras Mháirtín Uí Chadhain** (named after a well-known novelist and professor of Irish). This center operates under the auspices of the National University of Ireland, Galway. Send for a brochure: **Áras Mháirtín Uí Chadhain**, An Cheathrú Rua, Contae na Gaillimhe, Ireland. E-mail: arasuichadhain@tinet.ie

Or you may wish to get away from it all, to the smallest of the three Aran Islands in County Galway. Contact **Siarlinn Teo.**, Inis Oírr, Oileáin Árann, Contae na Gaillimhe, Ireland.

For those who wish to learn *Munster* Irish and enjoy the majestic landscape of the Dingle Peninsula, County Kerry, contact: **Oidhreacht Chorca Dhuibhne**, Baile an Fhirtéaraigh, Trá Lí, Contae Chiarraí, Ireland.

There is a small Gaeltacht in County Meath, less than an hour's drive from Dublin. Courses are available in County Meath. Write to: **Coláiste Eoghain Uí Ghramhnaigh**, Ráth Cairn, Contae na Mí, Ireland.

It would be invidious to suggest which course is the best. So, let us suggest you send for the **Oideas Gael** brochure and one other of your choice! If you do decide to attend a course in the Gaeltacht you may want to prepare yourself by using tapes or by familiarizing yourself with the world of Irish through the Internet. Information about **Bord na Gaeilge (Foras na Teanga)**, the state body to promote the Irish language, as well as details of language resources, can be found on: http://www.BnaG.ie.

There's a **chatline** in Irish on the Internet and maybe your soul mate is waiting to hear from you. He or she could be anywhere in the world: http://cgi-bin.iol.ie/cgi-bin/atlanticg.pl.

**Gaelic-L** is a Gaeltacht in cyberspace. If you would like to register as a citizen of this Gaeltacht, you will get a **céad míle fáilte**, a hundred thousand welcomes, by sending the order: **Subscribe Gaelic-L**, giving your name and your surname to: listserve@listserve.hea.

A company that designs, hosts and revises web pages on the Internet for Irish speakers is **Everson Gunn Teo**. They can be accessed at http://www.indigo.ie/egt/.

There are a number of CD Rom courses in Irish. Here are two:

**Learn Irish (Eurotalk)**, Eurotalk Ltd, 315 New King's Road, London SW6 4RF, U.K.

**Speakwrite Gaeilge,** Gal Mac Computers, Tuam Road, Galway, Ireland. As you begin to use one or more of these resource materials, you may like to take the odd plunge into the deep end and listen to storytellers, poets and singers on disc. Write for a catalogue to **Cló-Iar Chonnachta**, Indreabhán, Contae na Gaillimhe, Ireland.

Audio cassette courses are a popular way of learning, or brushing up on your Irish.

**Buntús Cainte**
Four audio cassettes and accompanying booklets of basic conversation (**Gael-Linn**).

**Cogar**
Four audio cassettes and booklet to bring you further along the road of basic conversational skills (**Gael-Linn**).

**Teach Yourself Irish**
by Diarmuid Ó Sé and Joseph Shiels with a pronunciation guide on
cassette (**Hodder & Stoughton**).

**The European Bureau for Lesser Used Languages**
The European Bureau for Lesser Used Languages has as its aim the
conservation and the promotion of lesser used autochthonous lan-
guages of the European Union.
Address: 10 Sráid Haiste Íocht., Baile Átha Cliath 2, Ireland.
Website: http://www.eblul.org

**The School of Celtic Studies**
The School of Celtic Studies is part of the Institute for Advanced
Studies, founded in 1940. Its publications are listed on the website:
http://www.dias.ie/celtic.html.

**Gaelscoileanna**
Gaelscoileanna is the umbrella organization for Irish-medium schools.
There are about 150 such schools in Ireland. Address: 7 Merrion
Square, Dublin 2.

# Abbreviations

| | |
|---|---|
| adj. | adjective |
| fem. | feminine |
| Gen. | Genitive |
| masc. | masculine |
| n. | noun |
| Nom. | Nominative |
| pl. | plural |
| sing. | singular |

# Irish Pronunciation

## THE IRISH ALPHABET

The letters of the Irish alphabet are:
**a b c d e f g h i l m n o p r s t u**

Words with the other letters of the Roman alphabet are loan words, such as **júdó** (judo), **quinín** (quinine), **zó-eolaí** (zoologist), etc. These words are listed in modern dictionaries.

## VOWELS

Vowels in Irish are either long or short.
Short vowels: **a, e, i, o, u**
Long vowels: **á, é, í, ó, ú**

Here are some words with the length accent on the vowel:
**smál** ( a stain, pronounced "small")
**pá** (pay, pronounced "paw")
**lá** (day, pronounced "law")
**bó** (cow, pronounced "bow, bow-knot")

All the above are long vowels. The following groups are also long:
**ae, ao, eo, omh(a), umh(a)**

*Examples:*
**Gael** (an Irish person, especially one identified with the Gaelic nation)
**caor** (a berry)

**feo** (decay)
**chomh** (adverb, as: in **chomh dearg le fuil** "as red as blood")
**comhairle** (advice, council)
**umhal** (humble)

## NASALISATION

Nasalisation is an important feature of Irish pronunciation. Some schoolchildren in Ireland don't seem to have a nose for it at all! What it means is allowing some of the breath to pass through the nose when uttering a word which has **m**, **n**, or **mh** before, or after, an accented vowel:
**máthair** (mother)
**comhairle** (advice, council)
**rón** (a seal)
**rún** (a secret)

## TONGUE POSITIONING

One raises the tip of the tongue quite a bit when pronouncing the short *i* in the following examples:
**fill** (to return)
**binn** (sweet-sounding)
**cait** (plural of **cat**, a cat)
**uimhir** (a number)
**coirce** (oats)
**doire** (an oak grove)

## THE MISSING VOWEL

The following letter combinations which are not preceded by a long vowel (**á, é, í, ó, ú**) are considered to have a missing vowel:
**lb, lbh, lf, lm**
**nb, nbh, nm**
**rb, rbh, rf, rg, rm**
Thus, **binb** (fury, venom) is pronounced as though it were spelt "binib." The grammatical term for this missing **i** is *epenthetic vowel*. An example of epenthesis in English is "elm." Irish people pronounce the word "film" as though it, too, had a missing **i**. When you hear the word spoken monosyllabically, you would guess the person was educated in England, or wished s(he) had been!

More examples of epenthesis:
**leanbh** (a child)
**airgead** (money)
**cealg** (deceit)

The tip of the tongue will also be quite high in the mouth when pronouncing words with long **i** (**í**) and words with **ao** or **aoi**.
**díreach** (straight)
**tír** (country)
**croí** (heart)
**buíoch** (thankful)
**cíoch** (breast)
**filíocht** (poetry)
**aon** (one)
**lao** (calf)
**aoire** (shepherd)
**baois** (folly)

The tip of the tongue halfway up:
You will find the tip of your tongue halfway up in the following combi-
nation of short vowels (**ei** and **ai**).
*Examples:*
**geimhreadh** (winter)
**seinm** (playing, of music)
**Meitheamh** (June)
**daibhir** (poor)

And in the following words with incorporation of long vowels (**é, éi, ae**):
**gé** (a goose)
**doiléir** (unclear)
**péist** (a worm)
**Béarla** (the English language)
**buidéal** (a bottle)
**contae** (a county)
**Gaeilge** (the Irish language)

Slightly raise the middle of the tongue:
Slightly raise the middle of the tongue for the following examples containing the short **a**:

**cam** (crooked)
**rann** (a verse)
**tobac** (tobacco)
**caint** (speech)
**cead** (permission)
**eaglais** (a church)
**peann** (a pen)
**beairic** (a barrack)
**saint** (greed)

And do the same for the following examples with a long **a** (**á**):
**bád** (a boat)
**lámh** (a hand)
**urlár** (a floor)
**Seán** (John)
**milseán** (a sweet)
**cáil** (fame, reputation)
**tiomáin** (drive)

The back of the tongue halfway up:
Raise the back of the tongue halfway when pronouncing the following examples containing the slender **o**:
**cnoc** (a hill)
**dorn** (a fist)
**bog** (soft)
**scoil** (school)
**droichead** (bridge)
**deoch** (a drink)
**sioc** (frost)

And in the following examples which are long (**ó, eo, omh**)
**cnó** (a nut)
**óg** (young)
**móin** (turf)
**deoir** (a drop)
**comharsa** (a neighbor)
**romhainn** (ahead of us, before us)

Raise the back of the tongue quite a bit:
You must raise the back of the tongue a bit more for the following words containing the short **u** and for the ending **adh**:
**luch** (a mouse)
**uncail** (an uncle)
**fliuch** (wet)
**samhradh** (summer)
**moladh** (praise)

And also for the following long **u** (**ú**) sounds and **umh**:
**cúng** (narrow)
**scrúdú** (examination)
**siúl** (walk)
**ciúin** (quiet)
**cumhacht** (power)
**cumhrán** (perfume)

The middle of the tongue halfway up:
Raise the middle of the tongue halfway up to pronounce words with a short **a** or **e** as in the following examples:
**cosantóir** (defender)
**póca** (pocket)
**binneas** (sweetness of sound)
**cailleach** (hag/witch)
**náire** (shame)

## EXERCISE AND REVISION

(i)
**im** (butter)
**pionta** (a pint)
**seachtain** (a week)
**miodóg** (a dagger)
Which part of the tongue goes where?
The tip of the tongue is raised quite a bit to handle the slender **i**.

(ii)
**ealaín** (art)

**buí** (yellow)
**claíomh** (a sword)
**deargadaol** (the devil's coach-horse)
Which part of the tongue goes where?
Yes, same as above, to handle the long **i** (**í**) and **ao**-sounds.

(iii)
What are you going to do with which part of your tongue for the following words?
**ceird** (a craft or trade)
**Beilgeach** (a Belgian)
**saibhreas** (wealth)
You will raise the tip of the tongue halfway up to deal with the short **ei** and **ai**.

And the following?
**inné** (yesterday)
**Coiscéim** (footstep; name of a publishing house)
**páipéar** (paper)
**aer** (air)
**ae** (liver)
You will do the same as above—tip of tongue, halfway up—to deal with the long **e** (**é**), **ei** and **ae**.

(v)
Now we come to a different part of the tongue. Which part, and how far is it raised?
**banríon** (a queen)
**barra** (crops)
**lathach** (mud)
**Aibreán** (April)
**aill** (a cliff)
**maitheas** (goodness)
The middle of the tongue is slightly raised to handle the short **a**.

(vi)
Now look at the next group:
**meáchan** (weight)
**ciseán** (a basket)
**barr** (top)

Yes, you've guessed it! Same as above, to deal with the long **a**. But, you say, how do I know **barr** is long? It doesn't have the length accent on the vowel. Yes, but **a** will be long if it comes before **rd** as in **ard** (high), **rl**, **rn** or before **rr** at the end of a word. So **barr** is long, as is **carr** (a car, a word with a Celtic root, incidentally).

(vi)
Now, if you can still move your tongue, we will go on to another group, for exercise and revision purposes.
**cos** (a foot)
**orlach** (an inch)
**eochair** (a key)
**gliomach** (a lobster)

What will you do with your tongue in this instance? Yes, you will raise the back of the tongue halfway to deal with the short **o** and **io** sounds.

(vii)
Now let's look at the long **ó** again and the long **eo**, **ói** and **omh**.
**fómhar** (autumn, fall, harvest)
**gnó** (business)
**brionglóid** (a dream)
**leoga!** (indeed! in Ulster Irish)
**Domhnach** (Sunday)

And, of course, you will do the same as you did above, raising the back of the tongue halfway.

We're nearly done with this revision. So, stick with it!

(viii)
What about this group of words, containing either a short **u** or **adh**:
**dubh** (black)
**subh** (jam)
**muc** (pig)
**guth** (voice)
**inniu** (today)
**tuilleadh** (more)

What do you do? Raise the back of the tongue quite a bit ...

And these?
**rásúr** (razor)
**breithiúnas** (judgment)
**saighdiúir** (soldier)
**pléisiúr** (pleasure)
**Mumhain** (Munster)

You did the same as in (viii), we hope. And why? To pronounce the long
**u** (**ú**) and **umh**.

(x)
Last bit of revision:
**anuas** (from above)
**portach** (bog)
**caite** (spent or worn out)
**gáire** (laughter)

What did you do with which part of your tongue, and why? The middle
of your tongue was raised halfway to deal with the short **a** and **e**.
God bless your tongue!

# Lesson 1: Greetings

| Seán: | **Dia dhuit!** |
|---|---|
| | Hello. (the usual form of greeting, literally: God be with you) |
| Máire: | **Dia is Muire dhuit!** |
| | Hello. (reply, literally: God and Mary with you!) |

| Seán: | **Dia is Muire dhuit!** |
|---|---|
| | Hello. (a more extended greeting) |
| Máire: | **Dia is Muire dhuit is Pádraig!** |
| | Hello. (reply, literally: God and Mary with you and Patrick!) |

While these greetings are used as unthinkingly as people may use "Hi!" or "Hello", they do underline a spiritual consciousness which pervades the language to this day.

| Éamonn: | **Bail ó Dhia ar an obair!** |
|---|---|
| | The blessing of God on the work! (the usual greeting to someone in the middle of work or some chore) |
| Muireann: | **An bhail chéanna ort!** |
| | The same blessing on you! (reply) |

### Other Greetings

**Go mbeannaí Dia dhuit!**　　　　God bless you!

A common expression, in Connaught Irish, when parting from someone: **Go ngnóthaí Dia dhuit!** May God prosper you! (**ngnóthaí** is pronounced *nú-í, nooey*)

Some common forms of greeting and farewell in letter-writing or e-mailing:
**A Chara**　　　　　　　　　Dear Sir/Madam (literally: O friend)

**A Áine dhil**             Dear Áine (informal address)
**Beatha agus Sláinte!** Life and Health! (a traditional opening to a letter)

Signing off:
**Beir bua agus beannacht**       Best wishes

A general greeting when joining a group, whether known to you or not:
**Bail ó Dhia oraibh!**         God bless you!

Call it superstition, if you like, but you should never comment on a
child in a pram or a baby in the cot without saying:
**Bail Ó Dhia air; bail ó Dhia uirthi!** God bless him; God bless her.

When someone sneezes, one says **Dia linn!** God with us.
For the second sneeze: **Dia linn is Muire!** God and Mary with us.
And so on, adding **Pádraig, Bríd** and **Colm Cille**. After which one says
**Capall bán fút!** Literally: A white horse under you.

As far as Irish is concerned, everything comes from God **ó Dhia**. Thus:
**Báisteach ó Dhia chugainn is gan é a bheith fliuch.**
Rain from God to us and may it not be wet.

**Is cuid an lae amárach go ndéana sé anocht!**
And tomorrow's share may it not be wet!


**GRAMMAR**

*Lenition*

The **séimhiú** is a softening of a consonant. In grammatical terms it is
called lenition.

In the nominative case, a feminine noun will be softened after the article:
**gealach**                 moon
**an ghealach**            the moon

**Chonaic mé an ghealach aréir.**    I saw the moon last night.

The lenition disappears in the genitive:
**solas na gealaí**                    the light of the moon

In the case of a masculine noun, there is no lenition in the nominative,
but it appears in the genitive:
**an bád**                             the boat
**dath an bháid**                      the color of the boat

Lenition occurs in the vocative, when addressing someone:
**cairde**                             friends
**a chairde**                          friends!
**diabhal**                            devil
**Tar anseo, a dhiabhail!**            Come here, you devil!

**mo** "my" and **do** "your" cause lenition:
**mála**                               bag
**Cá bhfuil mo mhála?**                Where is my bag?
**Tá do mhála sa chistin.**            Your bag is in the kitchen.

Lenition does not occur in the case of h, l, n, q, r, v, x, y, z or in the case
of s before c, f, m, p, t, v.

Adjectives following feminine nouns are softened:
**farraige**                           sea
**mór**                                great
**an fharraige mhór**                  the great sea

Verbs in the past or conditional will also be softened.
**bris**                               break
**Bhris mé an fhuinneog.**             I broke the window.
**Bhrisfeadh sé do chroí.**            It would break your heart.

Other instances of lenition include compound words:
**droch**                              bad
**bliain**                             year
**Drochbhliain ba ea í.**              It was a bad year.

**dea**                                good (+ hyphen)
**blasta**                             tasty
**Bhí béile dea-bhlasta agam aréir.**  I had a fine, tasty meal last night.

Let's look at the use of the word **go**. It is a verbal particle, used with the present subjunctive.

*Examples:*

| | |
|---|---|
| **Go dtaga do ríocht.** | Thy kingdom come. |
| **Go dtachta an diabhal thú.** | May the devil choke you. |
| **Go n-éirí leat.** | May you succeed. |
| **Go dtuga Dia foighne dom.** | May God give me patience. |
| **Go maire tú an céad.** | May you live to be a hundred. |
| **Go maire tú is go gcaithe tú é.** | May you live and wear it! (said to someone who has acquired something new). |
| **Go mbeirimid beo ar an am seo arís.** | May we live to see this time again! |
| **Go gcúití Dia leat é.** | May God reward you for it! |
| **Go bhfága Dia do shláinte agat.** | May God leave you your health (said when given something, i.e. a drink). |

### Word Order

Most simple Irish sentences follow the following word order:
verb + subject + object + other elements (adverb, adjective, etc.)

*Examples:*
**Chonaic mé dráma aréir.** I saw a play last night. (literally: Saw I a play last night.)

You will have noticed that there is no indefinite article in Irish: **dráma** is "a play."

Now we look at a longer sentence, with the same pattern repeated:

**D'éirigh (1) Tadhg (2) aréir (3) agus (4) chuaigh (5) ag fiach (6) giorraithe (7).** Tadhg (2) arose (1) last night (3) and (4) went (5) hunting (6) hares (7).

**Éireannach be ea mo mhamó.** My grandmother was Irish.
Note: **mamó** comes at the end in Irish and is softened after **mo**.

## LOOKING UP VOCABULARY

Use a dictionary to identify words you are not familiar with. But be careful: in the above examples, **go** has caused an eclipsis of letters (**urú** in Irish). If you look up the words **go gcúití Dia leat é** you will, of course, not find **gcúití** in the dictionary. Ignore the **g** and look for **cúitigh**, meaning "to compensate, reward, repay." Similarly, when identifying **go dtachta**, ignore the **d** and look for **tacht**; or **go bhfága**, ignore the **bh** and look for **fág.**

## NUMBERS

### Cardinal Numbers

| | | | |
|---|---|---|---|
| 1 | a haon | 11 | a haon déag |
| 2 | a dó | 12 | a dó dhéag |
| 3 | a trí | 13 | a trí déag |
| 4 | a ceathair | 14 | a ceathair déag |
| 5 | a cúig | 15 | a cúig déag |
| 6 | a sé | 16 | a sé déag |
| 7 | a seacht | 17 | a seacht déag |
| 8 | a hocht | 18 | a hocht déag |
| 9 | a naoi | 19 | a naoi déag |
| 10 | a deich | 20 | fiche (or scór) |

### Numbers with Nouns

| | |
|---|---|
| one horse | capall amháin |
| two horses | dhá chapall |
| three horses | trí chapall |
| four horses | ceithre chapall |
| five horses | cúig chapall |
| six horses | sé chapall |
| seven horses | seacht gcapall |
| eight horses | ocht gcapall |
| nine horses | naoi gcapall |
| ten horses | deich gcapall |
| twelve horses | dhá chapall déag |

There are some special plural forms, for example **trí bliana** (three years).

### Ordinal Numbers

| | |
|---|---|
| the first horse | **an chéad chapall** |
| the second ... | **an dara...** |
| the third... | **an tríú...** |
| the fourth... | **an ceathrú...** |
| the fifth... | **an cúigiú...** |
| the sixth... | **an séú...** |
| the seventh... | **an seachtú...** |
| the eighth... | **an t-ochtú...** |
| the ninth... | **an naoú...** |
| the tenth... | **an deichiú...** |

If a word starts with a vowel, such as the word **asal** (donkey), the ordinal numbers are:

| | |
|---|---|
| the first donkey | **an chéad asal** |
| the second (to tenth) | **an dara hasal** |

# Lesson 2: Introductions

Seosamh (Joseph) is visiting Ireland. He's talking to Laoise, who is from Ireland.

Seosamh: **Dia dhuit! Is mise Seosamh.**
Hello! I'm Joseph.

Laoise: **Dia is Muire dhuit, a Sheosaimh! Is mise Laoise. Cad as duit?**
Hello, Joseph. I'm Laoise. Where are you from?

Seosamh: **Is as Nua-Eabhrac dom. Éireannach ba ea mo mháthair. Ba as Ceatharlach di.**
I'm from New York. My mother was Irish. She was from Carlow.

Laoise: **Dáiríre?**
Really?

Seosamh: **Cad as duit féin?**
Where are you from yourself?

Laoise: **Ó, rugadh is tógadh san áit seo mé.**
Oh, I was born and raised here.

Seosamh: **Is deas an ait é an Daingean ...**
Dingle is a nice place ...

Laoise: **Is deas, is dócha. An raibh tú anseo cheana?**
It is, I suppose. Were you here before?

Seosamh: **Bhí ... tuairim is dhá bhliain ó shin.**
I was ... about two years ago.

## VOCABULARY

| | |
|---|---|
| Alaska | **Alasca** |
| Amsterdam | **Amstardam** |
| Athens | **An Aithin** |
| Australia | **An Astráil** |

| | |
|---|---|
| Austria | **An Ostair** |
| Belfast | **Béal Feirste** |
| Belgium | **An Bheilg** |
| Berlin | **Beirlín** |
| Boston | **Bostún** |
| Bristol | **Briostó** |
| Britain | **An Bhreatain** |
| Brittany | **An Bhriotáin** |
| Brussels | **An Bhruiséil** |
| Canada | **Ceanada** |
| Channel Islands | **Oileáin Mhuir nIocht** |
| China | **An tSín** |
| Connacht | **Cúige Chonnacht** |
| Cork | **Corcaigh** |
| Cornwall | **Corn na Breataine** |
| Denmark | **An Danmhairg** |
| Dublin | **Baile Átha Cliath** |
| Edinburgh | **Dún Éideann** |
| England | **Sasana** |
| Falkland Islands | **Oileáin Fháclainne (Na Malvinas)** |
| Finland | **An Fhionlainn** |
| France | **An Fhrainc** |
| Galway | **Gaillimh** |
| Germany | **An Ghearmáin** |
| Glasgow | **Glaschú** |
| Great Britain | **An Bhreatain Mhór** |
| Greece | **An Ghréig** |
| Greenland | **An Ghraonlainn** |
| Guernsey | **Geansaí** |
| Hebrides | **Inse Ghall** |
| Helsinki | **Heilsincí** |
| Iceland | **An Íoslainn** |
| Ireland | **Éire** |
| Israel | **Iosrael** |
| Italy | **An Iodáil** |
| Japan | **An tSeapáin** |
| Jersey | **Geirsí** |
| Jerusalem | **Iarúsailéim** |
| Korea | **An Chóiré** |

| | |
|---|---|
| Limerick | **Luimneach** |
| Liverpool | **Learpholl** |
| London | **Londain** |
| Madrid | **Maidrid** |
| Man, Isle of | **Manainn** |
| Manchester | **Manchain** |
| Moscow | **Moscó** |
| Munster | **Cúige Mumhan** |
| Netherlands | **An Ísiltír** |
| New Ireland | **Éire Nua** |
| New York | **Nua-Eabhrac** |
| New Zealand | **An Nua-Shéalainn** |
| Norway | **An Iorua** |
| Nova Scotia | **Albain Nua** |
| Orkneys | **Inse Orc** |
| Oslo | **Osló** |
| Ostend | **Ostainn** |
| Paris | **Páras** |
| Rome | **An Róimh** |
| Russia | **An Rúis** |
| Scotland | **Albain** |
| Shetland(s) | **Sealtainn** |
| South Africa | **An Afraic Theas** |
| Spain | **An Spáinn** |
| Sweden | **An tSualainn** |
| Switzerland | **An Eilvéis** |
| Tokyo | **Tóiceo** |
| Ulster | **Cúige Uladh** |
| United States of America (USA) | **Stáit Aontaithe Mheiriceá (SAM)** |
| Vatican City State | **Stát Chathair na Vatacáine** |
| Vienna | **Vín** |
| Wales | **An Bhreatain Bheag** |
| Waterford | **Port Láirge** |
| Wight, Isle of | **Inis Iocht** |
| York | **Eabhrac** |

## GRAMMAR

### *The Verb "to be"*

We use the copula "is" **is** and its negative "is not" **ní** to say someone or something is, or is not:

| | |
|---|---|
| **Is mise Seosamh.** | I'm Joseph. |
| **Is as an nGearmáin dom.** | I am from Germany. |
| **Is as an bhFrainc dom.** | I am from France. |
| **Is as an nGearmáin di.** | She is from Germany. |

| | |
|---|---|
| **Is as Ceanada dom.** | I am from Canada. |
| **... duit.** | You are from Canada. |
| **... dó.** | He is from Canada. |
| **... di.** | She is from Canada. |
| **... dúinn.** | We are from Canada. |
| **... daoibh.** | You (plural) are from Canada. |
| **... dóibh.** | They are from Canada. |

| | |
|---|---|
| **Ní mise Úna.** | I am not Úna. |

Apart from **is**, there is another form of the verb "to be": **tá**.

| | |
|---|---|
| **Tá sé fuar.** | It is cold. |
| **Tá sé dorcha.** | It is dark. |
| **Tá se déanach.** | It is late. |
| **Tá sí ag teacht.** | She is coming. |

### *Languages*

The word for Irish is **Gaeilge**. It is a feminine noun, **an Ghaeilge**.

| | |
|---|---|
| **Níl ach beagán Gaeilge agam.** | I only know (literally: have) a little Irish. |
| **Tá mé ag foghlaim na Gaeilge.** | I am learning Irish. |

The word for English is **Béarla**. It is a masculine noun. It is not soft-spoken in the nominative: **an Béarla**.

| | |
|---|---|
| **Ta mé ag foghlaim an Bhéarla.** | I am learning English. |

The article **an** does not change. The **b** becomes softened to a v-sound.

### *Place Names*

It helps, in a conversation, to know some place names. Irish place names are in the genitive if preceded by the County.

Cork - Corcaigh - Contae Chorcaí
Limerick - Luimneach - Contae Luimnigh
Dublin - Baile Átha Cliath - Contae Átha Cliath
Waterford - Port Láirge - Contae Phort Láirge

You will find a list of Irish towns, cities and other geographical features in the *Gazeteer of Ireland*.

### *Eclipse*

| | |
|---|---|
| the table | **an bord** |
| on the table | **ar an mbord** |

This change is called eclipse. This is how eclipse will change words beginning with **b, c, d, f, g, p, t: mb, gc, nd, bhf, ng, bp, dt.**

There is no eclipse in the case of words beginning with **h, l, m, n, q, r, s, v, x, y, z.**

We use eclipse for a direct object with the article followed by **ag**, for example:

| | |
|---|---|
| the man | **an fear** |
| that man has the money | **tá an t-airgead ag an bhfear** |

Prepositions which cause eclipse are **chuig, faoi, le, ó, roimh, thar, trí, um,** and **mura**, except when the noun begins with a **d** or a **t**.

Don't give up! It will all become easy with familiarity.

*Some examples:*
**faoi + an = faoin**
**Tá an leabhar faoin mbord.**          The book is under the table.

Note the eclipse of **bord**. The original b-sound in **bord** is lost and is replaced by the sound of the eclipse.

**do + an = don**
**Thug mé don fhear sin é.**          I gave it to that man.
Notice the softening (lenition) of **fear** (To complicate matters, Munster speakers prefer eclipse: **don bhfear**).

### *Simple Prepositions with the Definite Article*

#### With Singular Noun
ar + an = ar an
de + an = den
do + an = don
faoi + an = faoin
ó + an = ón
roimh + an = roimh an
thar + an = thar an
trí + an = tríd an
ag + an = ag an
as + an = as an
chuig + an = chuig an
i + an = sa (before consonant)
         sna (before vowel)
         san (before f + vowel)

#### With Plural Noun
ar na = ar na
de + na = de na
do + an = do na
faoi + na = faoi na
ó na = ó na
roimh na = roimh na
thar na = thar na
trí na = trí na
ag na = ag na
as na = as na
chiug + na = chuig na
sa + na = sna

*Examples:*
sa + an + áit = **san áit**          in the place
trí + an = **tríd an ngeata**        through the gate
faoi + an = **faoin gcathaoir**      under the chair

## Nouns

Nouns in Irish are either masculine or feminine. Here are some examples:

| Feminine Nouns | | Masculine Nouns | |
|---|---|---|---|
| **abhainn** | river | **bád** | boat |
| **bean** | woman | **fear** | man |
| **farraige** | sea | **leabhar** | book |
| **gaoth** | wind | **mac** | son |
| **long** | ship | **oileán** | island |
| **nead** | nest | **ór** | gold |
| **oíche** | night | **rón** | seal (mammal) |
| **tine** | fire | **teach** | house |
| **traein** | train | **uan** | lamb |

Only by usage will you learn the difference but here are some ways of recognizing masculine nouns.

Examples for different noun endings:
-**ín: cailín** girl; **frídín** germ; **pincín** minnow
-**án: amhrán** song; **amadán** fool; **árasán** apartment
-**úr: casúr** hammer; **pionsúr** pincers; **seamsúr** chanter (pipes)
-**ún: náisiún** nation; **bastún** lout; **príosún** prison
-**óir/eoir: bainisteoir** manager; **fiaclóir** dentist; **ceoltóir** musician
-**(a)ire: mangaire** hawker; **iascaire** fisherman; **druilire** drill
-**(i)úir: táilliúir** tailor; **dochtúir** doctor, **saighdiúir** soldier
-**éir: siúinéir** carpenter; **báicéir** baker; **úinéir** owner
-**(a)í: scríobhaí** scribe; **náibhí** navy; **oibrí** worker

Some ways of recognizing feminine nouns:

A noun ending with:
-**óg/-eog: seamróg** shamrock; **poibleog** poplar; **fuinneog** window
-**(i)úint: canúint** dialect; **oiliúint** training; **giniúint** procreation
-**lann: leabharlann** library; **bialann** restaurant; **amharclann** theater

Also feminine are words of more than one syllable ending with -(e)acht: **éisteacht** hearing; **clisteacht** cleverness.

The definite article **an** lenites the initial consonant of feminine nouns:

| | |
|---|---|
| **an fhuinneog** | the window |
| **an fharraige** | the sea |

This happens always, except in the case of feminine nouns beginning with **d** and **t**:

| | |
|---|---|
| **an díle** | the flood |
| **an tine** | the fire |

### The Genitive

The Genitive is important in Irish and has many uses. Masculine and feminine nouns will behave differently in the genitive. The genitive may indicate origin:
**ubh lachan** a duck egg — **lachan** being the genitive of **lacha** a duck.

It may indicate ownership:
**scuab an ealaíontóra** the artist's brush — **ealaíontóra** being the genitive of **ealaíontóir** an artist.

It may indicate the material:
**bréagán adhmaid** a wooden toy — **adhmaid** being the genitive of **adhmad** wood.

It may indicate position:
**roth tosaigh** front wheel — **tosaigh** being the genitive of **tosach** front.

It can indicate a profession:
**fear an bhainne** the milkman — Notice the change from the unlenited nominative **an bainne** the milk.

It can be used to describe a condition:
**lá báistí** a rainy day — **báistí** being the genitive of **báisteach** rain.

It can indicate use:
**capall ualaigh** a pack-horse — **ualaigh** being the genitive of **ualach** a load.

It may indicate value:
**stampa pingine** a penny stamp — **pingine** being the genitive of **pingin** a penny.

It may indicate measurement or time:
**leanbh míosa** a month-old baby — **míosa** being the genitive of **mí** a month.

It also indicates relationships:
**col fola** consanguinity — **fola** being the genitive of **fuil** blood.

Other uses are quantity:
**roinnt ime** some butter — **ime** being the genitive of **im** butter.

The genitive is required when speaking of a container or what it holds:
**bosca lasán** a box of matches — **lasán** being the genitive plural of **lasán** a match.

You will also need the genitive after the comparative form of the adjective:
**níos mó céille** more sense — **céille** being the genitive of **ciall** sense.

You will see it in street names and place names:
**Lána na Trá** Beach Lane — **na trá** being the genitive of **an trá** the beach.

The genitive will follow **ag**:
**ag cur allais** sweating — **allais** being the genitive of **allas** sweat.

The genitive also follows such words in prepositional phrases as:
**timpeall an tí** around the house — **tí** being the genitive of **teach** house.
**trasna an bhóthair** across the road — nominative: **an bóthar**.
**ag guí chun Dé** praying to God — nominative: **Dia**.

## *Declensions*

Nouns are divided into five declensions. The table shows their endings:

|  | Ending of Nom. Sing. | Ending of Gen. Sing. | Example |
|---|---|---|---|
| **First** | Broad consonant | Slender consonant | bád/báid (boat) |
| **Second** | Consonant | -e, -í | cos/coise (leg) curach/curái (curragh) |
| **Third** | Consonant | -a | ab/aba (abbot) |
| **Fourth** | Consonant or vowel | No change | rí/rí (king) pillín/pillín (pad) |
| **Fifth** | Slender consonant or vowel | Broad consonant | lacha/lachan (duck) bráid/brád (neck) |

First Declension

All the following nouns are masculine, ending with a broad consonant **-adh, -án, -ch, -éad, -éal, -éan, -éar, -s, -ún, -úr**: (some **-ch** endings are feminine: see second declension):

| | |
|---|---|
| **geimhreadh** | winter |
| **leannán** | lover |
| **móinteach** | moorland |
| **firéad** | ferret |
| **painéal** | panel |
| **fíréan** | just person |
| **áiléar** | loft, gallery |
| **gríos** | hot ashes |
| **rún** | secret |
| **iúr** | yew |

Second Declension

The vast majority of these nouns are feminine, ending with a consonant, as in **-ch, -ilt, -is, -lann, -óg**:

| | |
|---|---|
| **beach** | bee |
| **fuascailt** | deliverance, solution |
| **Seicis** | Czech (language) |
| **otharlann** | infirmary |
| **barróg** | embrace |

Third Declension
Ending with a consonant, this is a mixed bag. Firstly we have feminine nouns ending with -acht and some with the same ending that are masculine:
feminine: **mallacht** curse; **léacht** lecture
masculine: **tocht** mattress; **locht** fault

Secondly we have feminine nouns of more than one syllable ending with -áil, -áint, -áint, -chan, -íl, -irt, -úil, -úint:

| | |
|---|---|
| cadráil | gossip |
| cosaint | defense |
| tiomáint | driving |
| athnuachan | renewal |
| búiríl | bellowing |
| íobairt | sacrifice |
| barúil | opinion |
| canúint | dialect |

Thirdly we have masculine nouns of more than one syllable ending in -aeir, -éir, -eoir, -úir:

| | |
|---|---|
| foghlaeir | fowler |
| péintéir | painter |
| iomaitheoir | competitor |
| ionróir | invader |
| táilliúir | tailor |

Fourth Declension
Mostly ending with a vowel, some with a consonant. Usually these are words describing people or their professions, usually masculine, ending with -a, -í, -ire:

| | |
|---|---|
| méara | mayor |
| rí | king |
| gliaire | gladiator |

Nouns ending with -ín, the vast majority of which are masculine:

| | |
|---|---|
| cailín | girl |
| duinín | homunculus |
| dúidín | clay pipe |
| coinín | rabbit |

Also in the Fourth Declension and usually feminine are abstract nouns:

| | |
|---|---|
| **amaidí** | folly |
| **easpa** | absence, lack |
| **maoile** | bareness |

Two final categories belonging to the Fourth Declension are masculine nouns ending with a consonant:

| | |
|---|---|
| **máistir** | master |
| **bus** | bus |

Finally, most nouns ending in **-e**, whether masculine or feminine:

| | |
|---|---|
| **gloine** | glass |
| **fine** | family group, race |
| **buime** | foster mother, nurse |

Fifth Declension

Usually feminine, ending with a consonant or with a vowel:

| | |
|---|---|
| **lasair** | flame (fem.) |
| **cara** | friend (masc.) |

### *Nouns in the Genitive*

First Declension

Slenderize the nominative singular to form the genitive singular.

| Nom. Sing | Gen. Sing. | Nom. Pl. | Gen. Pl. | English |
|---|---|---|---|---|
| geimhreadh | geimhridh | geimhrí | geimhrí | winter |
| leannán | leannáin | leannáin | leannán | lover |
| móinteach | móintigh | móintigh | móinteach | moorland |
| firéad | firéid | firéid | firéad | ferret |
| painéal | painéil | painéil | painéal | panel |
| gríos | grís | — | — | hot ashes |
| rún | rúin | rúin | rúin | secret/darling |
| iúr | iúir | iúir | iúr | yew |

See what happens, now, with the definite article included:
**an firéad** the ferret; **cos an fhiréid** the ferret's foot; **na firéid** the ferrets;
**boladh na bhfiréad** the smell of the ferrets.


## Second Declension

| Nom. Sing. | Gen. Sing. | Nom. Pl. | Gen. Pl. | English |
|------------|------------|----------|----------|---------|
| beach | beiche | beacha | beach | bee |
| fuascailt | fuascailte | fuascailtí | fuascailtí | release |
| otharlann | otharlainne | otharlanna | otharlann | infirmary |
| barróg | barróige | barróga | barróg | embrace |


Example with the article:
**cealg na beiche**          the bee's sting
**cealg na mbeach**        the bees' sting

## Third Declension

| Nom. Sing. | Gen. Sing. | Nom. Pl. | Gen. Pl. | English |
|------------|------------|----------|----------|---------|
| mallacht | mallachta | mallachtaí | mallachtaí | curse |
| léacht | léachta | léachtaí | léacht | lecture |
| tocht | tochta | tochtanna | tochtanna | mattress |
| cadráil | cadrála | — | — | gossip |
| cosaint | cosanta | — | — | defense |
| tiomáint | tiomána | — | — | driving |
| búiríl | búiríola | — | — | bellowing |
| íobairt | íobartha | íobairtí | íobairtí | sacrifice |
| barúil | barúla | barúlacha | barúlacha | opinion |
| canúint | canúna | canúintí | canúintí | dialect |

| Nom. Sing. | Gen. Sing. | Nom. Pl. | Gen. Pl. | English |
|---|---|---|---|---|
| foghlaeir | foghlaera | foghlaeirí | foghlaeirí | fowler |
| péintéir | péintéara | péintéirí | péintéirí | painter |
| iomaitheoir | iomaitheora | iomaitheoirí | iomaitheoirí | competitor |
| ionróir | ionróra | ionróirí | ionróirí | invader |
| táilliúir | táilliúra | táilliúirí | táilliúirí | tailor |

Examples with the article:

**uigeacht an tochta**  the texture of the mattress (masc.)
**tús an hathnuachana**  the beginning of the renewal (fem.)

Fourth Declension

| Nom. Sing. | Gen. Sing. | Nom. Pl. | Nom. Pl. | English |
|---|---|---|---|---|
| méara | méara | méaraí | méaraí | mayor |
| rí | rí | ríthe | ríthe | king |
| gliaire | gliaire | gliairí | gliairí | gladiator |
| cailín | cailín | cailíní | cailíní | girl |
| duinín | duinín | duiníní | duiníní | homunculus |
| máistir | máistir | máistrí | máistrí | master |

Some examples with the article:

**hata an chailín**  the girl's hat
**misneach na ngliairí**  the courage of the gladiators

Fifth Declension

| Nom. Sing. | Gen. Sing. | Nom. Pl. | Gen. Pl. | English |
|---|---|---|---|---|
| lasair | lasrach | lasracha | lasracha | flame |
| cara | carad | cairde | cairde/carad | friend |

Examples with (a) article and (b) possessive adjective:

**dath na lasrach**                     the color of the flame
**teach mo charad**                     my friend's house

## EXERCISE

From their endings, determine whether the following nouns are masculine or feminine:

| | |
|---|---|
| **síbín** | speakeasy |
| **sicín** | chicken |
| **stiléir** | distiller |
| **doirseoir** | door keeper |
| **rásúr** | razor |
| **bábóg** | doll |
| **castán** | sweet chestnut |
| **cinniúint** | destiny |
| **pictiúrlann** | cinema |
| **mathún** | bear |
| **feadaire** | whistler |
| **ionadaí** | representative |

I hope you got 100% in that little exercise!

# Lesson 3: Talking on the Phone

Seosamh rings Laoise. He'd like to get her out to a pub. There's a good musical session on tomorrow night.

Seosamh: **An bhféadfainn labhairt le Laoise, le do thoil?**
May I speak with Laoise, please?

Laoise: **Laoise ag caint. Cé atá agam?**
Laoise speaking. Who is this?

Seosamh: **Níor aithníos do ghlór. Seosamh anseo. Cogar, ar mhaith leat dul amach istoíche amárach?**
I didn't recognize your voice. Seosamh here. Tell me, would you like to go out tomorrow night?

Laoise: **Istoíche amárach? Níl a fhios agam ...**
Tomorrow night? I don't know ...

Seosamh: **Beidh Altan ag seinm sa Chrúiscín Folamh.**
Altan will be playing in The Empty Jug.

Laoise: **Taitníonn Altan liom. Ach ní thaitníonn An Crúiscín Folamh liom. Bíonn sé róghlórach.**
I like Altan. But I don't like The Empty Jug. It's too noisy.

Seosamh: **Bíonn is dócha. Níl fonn amach ort mar sin?**
It is, I suppose. You don't feel like going out so?

Laoise: **Níl. Oíche éigin eile b'fhéidir.**
No, some other night, maybe.

Seosamh: **Tá go maith. Glaoigh orm má thagann athrú aigne ort. An bhfuil m'uimhir agat?**
O.K. Call me if you change your mind. Do you have my number?

Laoise: **Tá! Slán!**
I do! Bye!

**Slán!** is short for **Go dté tú slán** Fare thee well.

## GRAMMAR

### The Verb "to know"

| | |
|---|---|
| I don't know. | **Níl a fhios agam.** |
| He does not know. | **Níl a fhios aige.** |
| She does not know. | **Níl a fhios aici.** |

### Negation

We have a choice of using two forms of the verb here:

Seosamh says: **Ar mhaith leat dul amach?** Would you like to go out?
The answer is: **Ba mhaith liom** "I would" or **Níor mhaith** "I would not."

Another example:
I did not hit the dog. **Níor bhuaileas an madra.** or **Níor bhuail mé an madra.**

### Possessive Pronouns

*Examples:*
Seosamh says: **Níor aithníos do ghlór.**
                    I didn't recognize your voice!

| | |
|---|---|
| I didn't recognize her voice. | **Níor aithníos a glór.** |
| I didn't recognize his voice. | **Níor aithníos a ghlór.** |

### Relative Clauses

Relative clauses require the use of a relative particle. They fall into two categories, the direct relative and the indirect relative:

(a) Direct Relative
It lenites the initial consonant of all verbs (with the exception of **tá**, **deir** and **fuair**).

**an fhuinneog a bhris an buachaill** the window which the boy broke
**an dlúthdhiosca a dhíol mo dhearthair** the CD which my brother sold
**an bhean a chaill a mála** the woman who lost her bag

(b) Indirect Relative
**an fear a bhfuil a iníon san ospidéal**
the man whose daughter is in the hospital
**an cailín a dtugaim punt di gach lá**
the girl to whom I give a pound every day
**an cailín ar thugas punt di anuraidh**
the girl to whom I gave a pound last year

The form **ní fios** can be used this way:
**Ní fios cé a chum an dán.**
It is not known who wrote the poem.


## Conditional Sentences

Seosamh says: **Glaoigh orm má ...**     Call me if ...

**Má éiríonn liom a bheith i mBaile Átha Cliath, cuirfidh mé glao ort.**
If I manage to be in Dublin, I'll give you a ring.


## Approximation

**Éigin** can be used to denote approximation.
Note: in Connaught Irish, **éigin** is often pronounced *eicínt*.

*Examples:*
**céad éigin dollar**                 a hundred dollars or so
Laoise takes a rain check by saying:
**Oíche éigin eile ...**              Some other night...
**Uair éigin sna fichidí a tharla sé ...**
It happened some time in the twenties ...
**some fine day ...**                 lá breá éigin ...

In reference to something that is unlikely to happen for some time, we say:

**Béarfaidh bó éigin, lao éigin, lá éigin.**
Some cow will give birth to some calf some day.

## PROVERBS AND SAYINGS

**Cosa gloine fúibh — is go mbrise siad!**
Glass legs under you — and may they break!
*Said to hens.*

**Nár mhúcha Dia solas na bhFlaitheas orainn!**
May God not quench the light of Heaven on us!
*Said when putting out the light at night.*

**Is olc an t-éan a shalaíonn a nead féin.**
It's a bad bird that fouls its own nest.

**Níor dhún Dia doras riamh nár oscail sé ceann eile.**
God never closed a door without opening another.

**Cad a dhéanfadh mac an chait ach luch a mharú!**
What would the cat's son do but kill a mouse!
*Like father, like son.*

**An t-aonú aithne dhéag — tabhair aire duit féin!**
The eleventh commandment — look after yourself!

**Tabhair an mhóin abhaile agus cuirfidh mise tine mhór síos.**
Bring home the turf and I'll light a big fire.

**Ag breith liúdar go Toraigh.**
Bringing coalfish to Tory.
*Bringing coal to Newcastle.*

**Téann an bainne sa gheimhreadh go hadharca na mbó.**
In winter the milk goes to the cows' horns.

**Chomh gaelach le muca Dhroichead Átha.**
As Irish as the pigs of Drogheda.

**Ní dheachaigh Harry Stottle amach oíche fhómhair.**
Aristotle never went out on an autumn night.

**Codladh an ghiorria.**          The sleep of a hare.
                                  *With one eye open.*

**Is minic a bhris béal duine a shrón.**
A person's mouth often broke his nose.

**Bhearrfadh sé luch ina codladh!**
He'd shave a sleeping mouse!

**Na trí glórtha is binne:**      The three sweetest sounds:
**Meilt bhró**                    Quern-stone grinding,
**Géimneach bó,**                 Cow lowing,
**Béic linbh.**                   Child screaming.

**Ag cur claí timpeall goirt leis an gcuach a choinneáil istigh.**
Putting a fence around the field to keep in the cuckoo.

**Chomh díomhaoin le ladhraicín píobaire.**
As idle as a piper's little finger.

**Is minic táilliúir agus drochthreabhsar air,**
**Is minic gréasaí agus drochbhróga faoi.**
Often a tailor with bad trousers,
Often a cobbler with bad shoes.

**Maireann croí éadrom i bhfad.**   The light heart lives long.

**Gach éan mar a oiltear**          Every bird as it is brought up
**Agus an naosc san abar.**         And the snipe in the mud.

**Luimneach a bhí,**               Limerick that was,
**Baile Átha Cliath atá,**         Dublin that is,
**Corcaigh a bheidh!**             Cork that will be!

**Chomh sleamhain le bolg eascainne.**
As slippery as an eel's belly.

**Chomh pioctha le sagart.**
As neat as a priest.

**Chomh ramhar le ministir.**
As plump as a minister.

**Chomh sámh le liopadaileap.**
As tranquil as a basking shark.

**Chomh caoch le bonn mo bhróige.**
As blind as the sole of my shoe.

**Chomh casta le hadharc reithe.**
As crooked as a ram's horn.

**Chomh hata le frog san fhómhar.**
As swollen as a frog in autumn.

**Chomh géar-radharcach le gainéad.**
As sharp-sighted as a gannet.

**Chomh díreach is atá an chnámh i ndroim na lachan.**
As straight as the bone in the duck's back.

**Chomh bocht le bairneach.**
As poor as a limpet.

**Chomh bréan le pluais an mhadra rua.**
As smelly as a fox's den.

**Is minic cú mall sona.**
A slow hound is often happy.

**An rud nach féidir ní féidir é.**
What can't be done can't be done.

**Ní críonnacht creagaireacht.**
Miserliness is not thrift.

**Is iomaí duine ag Dia.**
It takes all sorts to make a world.

**Léim ón tine chun na gríosaí.**
Leaping from the fire to the hot ashes.
*(Out of the frying-pan into the fire.)*

**Más fada an lá tig an oíche.**
Though the day be long, night will come.
*(Everything comes to an end.)*

**Éist mórán agus can beagán.**
Hear much and say little.

**Den duine an t-éadach.**
Clothes make the person.

**Is deacair an drochrud a mharú.**
It's hard to kill a bad thing.

**Tabhair póg do chos an ghiorria.**
Kiss the leg of the hare.
*(Say goodbye to something that's lost for ever.)*

**Cuir síoda ar ghabhar agus is gabhar i gcónaí é.**
Put silk on a goat and it's still a goat.

**Is glas iad na cnoic i bhfad uainn.**
Faraway hills are green.

**Bíonn adharca fada ar na ba thar lear.**
Foreign cows have long horns.

**Is minic a rinne bromach gioblach capall cumasach.**
Many a ragged colt made a noble horse.

**Mair, a chapaill, agus gheobhaidh tú féar.**
Live, horse, and you will get grass.

**Is fearr cairde ná ór.**
Friends are better than gold.

**Níl aon tinteán mar do thinteán féin.**
There's no hearth like your own hearth.
*(There's no place like home.)*

**Ná díol do chearc lá fliuch.**
Don't sell your hen on a wet day.


**FURTHER READING**

*Irish Proverbs in Irish and English* by Gabriel Rosenstock, (Mercier
     Press, 1999).

# Lesson 4: Courtesies

Séan: **Gabh mo leithscéal, cá bhfuil teach an asail le do thoil?**
Excuse me, where is the toilet*, please?
Máire: **Nach bhfeiceann tú os do chomhair é — an doras a bhfuil Fir scríofa air.**
Can't you see it in front of you there — the door with Gents written on it.
Séan: **Feicim anois é — go raibh maith agat.**
I see it now — thank you.
Máire: **Tá fáilte romhat!**
You are welcome!

*The words "bathroom" and "restroom" sound somewhat American to Irish ears. A common term for "toilet" in the Gaeltacht is **teach an asail** the donkey's house.

## VOCABULARY

Basic courtesies are necessary when acquiring a language. You start off on the right foot by showing sensitivity. The Irish language is full of phrases employed to thank people, encourage people or praise people.

| | |
|---|---|
| **Más é do thoil é.** | Please. (literally: if it is your will) |
| **Mura miste leat.** | If you don't mind. |
| **Gabh mo leithscéal.** | Excuse me. |
| **Go raibh míle maith agat!** | Thanks. (literally: a thousand thanks) |
| **Dia sa teach!** | God bless all here. (a traditional exclamation on entering an Irish-speaking house, literally: God in the house) |
| **Go sábhála Dia sinn!** | God save us! |

One of the worst things you could say to anybody is **Nár fheice tú Dia**
"May you not see God." So, even if you are an atheist, you will have to
accept that God is central to basic communication in Irish!

## GRAMMAR

### *Prepositional Phrases*

In front of
| | |
|---|---|
| **os mo chomhair** | in front of me |
| **os do chomhair** | in front of you |
| **os a comhair** | in front of her |
| **os a chomhair** | in front of him |
| **os bhur gcomhair** | in front of you (pl.) |
| **os ár gcomhair** | in front of us |
| **os a gcomhair** | in front of them |

### *Past Tense*

Laoise asked Seosamh was he in Dingle before. He replied by using the
past tense of **tá** which is **bhí**.

| | |
|---|---|
| **An raibh tú anseo cheana?** | Were you here before? |
| **Bhí ... tuairim is dhá bhliain ó shin.** | Yes ... about two years ago. |
| **Éireannach ba ea mo mhamó/ mo dhaideo.** | My grandmother/grandfather was Irish. |

### *Regular Verbs*

What do we mean by independent, dependent and autonomous forms
of the verb? Let us take the verb **déan** "to do."

| | |
|---|---|
| Independent: | **rinne** |
| Dependent: | **dearna (dhearna/ndearna)** |
| Autonomous: | **rinneadh** |

*Examples*

| | |
|---|---|
| **Rinne sé é.** | He did it. |
| **Ní dhearna sé é.** | He did not do it. |
| **Rinneadh é.** | It was done. |

You will notice that the last example does not specify the doer. That is what we mean by the autonomous form. The independent form is the ordinary, straightforward form of the verb. It becomes dependent only when we put a verbal particle before it, i.e. **ní, go, nach, an.**

Examples of the dependent form:

| | |
|---|---|
| **An ndearna sé é?** | Did he do it? |
| **Dúirt sé go ndearna sé é.** | He said he did it. |
| **Dúirt sé nach ndearna sé é.** | He said he did not do it. |
| **Ní dhearna sé é.** | He did not do it. |

Present

| **molaim (mol)** praise | | **brisim (bris)** break | |
|---|---|---|---|
| *Sing.* | *Pl.* | *Sing.* | *Pl.* |
| 1. molaim | molaimid | brisim | brisimid |
| 2. molann tú | molann sibh | briseann tú | briseann sibh |
| 3. molann sé | molann siad | briseann sé | briseann siad |
| *Autonomous* | | *Autonomous* | |
| moltar | | bristear | |

Past Tense

| **molaim (mol)** praise | | **brisim (bris)** break | |
|---|---|---|---|
| *Sing.* | *Pl.* | *Sing.* | *Pl.* |
| 1. mhol mé | mholamar | bhris mé | bhriseamar |
| 2. mhol tú | mhol sibh | bhris tú | bhris sibh |
| 3. mhol sé | mhol siad | bhris sé | bhris siad |
| *Autonomous* | | *Autonomous* | |
| moladh | | briseadh | |

## Past Habitual

| molaim (mol) praise | | brisim (bris) break | |
|---|---|---|---|
| *Sing.* | *Pl.* | *Sing.* | *Pl.* |
| 1. mholainn | mholaimis | bhrisinn | bhrisimis |
| 2. mholtá | mholadh sibh | bhristeá | bhriseadh sibh |
| 3. mholadh sé | mholaidís | bhriseadh sé | bhrisidís |
| *Autonomous* | | *Autonomous* | |
| mholtaí | | bhristí | |

## Future

| molaim (mol) praise | | brisim (bris) break | |
|---|---|---|---|
| *Sing.* | *Pl.* | *Sing.* | *Pl.* |
| 1. molfaidh mé | molfaimid | brisfidh mé | brisfimid |
| 2. molfaidh tú | molfaidh sibh | brisfidh tú | brisfidh sibh |
| 3. molfaidh sé | molfaidh siad | brisfidh sé | brisfidh siad |
| *Autonomous* | | *Autonomous* | |
| molfar | | brisfear | |

## Conditional

| molaim (mol) praise | | brisim (bris) break | |
|---|---|---|---|
| *Sing.* | *Pl.* | *Sing.* | *Pl.* |
| 1. mholfainn | mholfaimis | bhrisfinn | bhrisfimis |
| 2. mholfá | mholfadh sibh | bhrisfeá | bhrisfeadh sibh |
| 3. mholfadh sé | mholfaidís | bhrisfeadh sé | bhrisfidís |
| *Autonomous* | | *Autonomous* | |
| mholfaí | | bhrisfí | |

## Present Subjunctive

| molaim (mol) praise | | brisim (bris) break | |
|---|---|---|---|
| *Sing.* | *Pl.* | *Sing.* | *Pl.* |
| 1. mola mé | molaimid | brise mé | brisimid |
| 2. mola tú | mola sibh | brise tú | brise sibh |
| 3. mola sé | mola siad | brise sé | brise siad |
| *Autonomous* | | *Autonomous* | |
| moltar | | bristear | |

## Imperative

| molaim (mol) praise | | brisim (bris) break | |
|---|---|---|---|
| *Sing.* | *Pl.* | *Sing.* | *Pl.* |
| 1. molaim | molaimis | brisim | brisimis |
| 2. mol | molaigí | bris | brisigí |
| 3. moladh sé | molaidís | briseadh sé | brisidís |
| *Autonomous* | | *Autonomous* | |
| moltar | | bristear | |

## Verbal Noun

| molaim (mol) praise | brisim (bris) break |
|---|---|
| moladh | briseadh |

## Verbal Adjective

| molaim (mol) praise | brisim (bris) break |
|---|---|
| molta | briste |

**EXERCISE**

I broke the bottle. **Bhris mé an buidéal.**
How would you say: "He will break the bottle"?

Go to the Future (above) and the third person singular: **Brisfidh sé
an buidéal.**
Now, how would you say, "The bottle will be broken"?

Go to the Future again; this time to the autonomous form: **Brisfear an
buidéal.**


**DINNEENISMS!**

Pádraig Ó Duinnín (1860-1934) was a Kerry-born Jesuit, often seen
emerging from the National Library with manuscripts stuffed under a
snuff-peppered cassock. He compiled an Irish-English Dictionary (Irish
Texts Society, London) which is still a desert-island choice for many Irish
people, if faced with being only allowed one book for an indefinite period.
The text is in 'cló Gaelach' or Irish font, with the lenition on consonants
indicated by a dot, rather than the modern 'h'. Much of the spelling has
been modernised or simplified in subsequent dictionaries.

Even though you may be a mere beginner in Irish, you can impress and
delight Irish speakers with your knowledge of arcane Dinneenisms,
many of which have been expunged from modern dictionaries.

**aingeal**—an angel; or a burnt-out cinder taken from the fire, some-
    times given to children going out at night to carry as a talisman or
    protection.

**amadáinín**—a little fool; or a tool to beat the soil around plants.

**amanairis**—the second day after tomorrow.

**bearadóir**—one who probes for bog wood by means of an iron bar or
    spike with a wooden handle. The prober having then stuck the bar
    into the bog applies his teeth to the timber handle to detect bog wood.

**bearradóir**—(not to be confused with the above) a cow that eats the hair of her tail or of other cow's tails.

**buarach bháis**—used in witchcraft, an unbroken hoop of skin cut from a corpse while reciting incantations. The piece, the length of the entire body from shoulder to foot sole, is then wrapped in silk of the colors of the rainbow. It is used to tie the legs of a person to produce certain special effects.

**céad**—means a hundred but **céad éisc** was 128 fish (in Kerry) and while **bannlámh** was a measure of 21 inches of home-made cloth, it was 24 inches in West Kerry; we hope you do not encounter fleas in Ireland but if you do you may—if your conscience permits—try the **ciorrú má gcuach** which is an all-round mangling of a flea between thumb and forefinger!

**codam**—a swelling of the gums of horses that are fed on furze.

**Donn**—among other things, the name of a fairy inhabiting sandbanks off the Clare coast.

**drúichtín**—a small pale slug or snail. On May mornings girls examined the shade of coloring of the first drúichtín they encountered to discover the color of their future husband's hair.

**gabhairín**—a little goat; or potatoes sold secretly by children for pocket money.

**gealach**—not only the moon, or brightness, but also the white circle in a slice of half-boiled potato or turnip; also denotes frenzy, or madness.

**géiríní**—a tailor's leavings after the garment is cut.

**iomas gréine**—sun-inspiration or a sun-bubble formed on herbs, bestowing the gift of poetry to the eater.

**púcán**—the sod in a shallow pool.

**sagairtín**—a little priest or an inedible periwinkle.

**seala**—an ancient measure–a ration of four eggfuls of honey.

**seicimínín**—the belly skin that falls down between the legs of well-fed geese.

**sleith**—a term in Brehon Law, signifying intercourse with a woman without her consent or knowledge.

**ullastráth**—the day before the day before yesterday.

# Lesson 5: Directions

Séan: **Gabh mo leithscéal. Níl ach beagán Gaeilge agam. Cá bhfuil An Gliomach Buile, le do thoil?**
Excuse me. I only know a little Irish. Where is the Mad Lobster, please?

Máire: **Níl tú i bhfad uaidh. Téigh díreach ar aghaidh. Cas ar chlé, ansin an dara casadh ar dheis. Tá An Gliomach Buile os comhair an tséipéil.**
You're not far from it. Go straight ahead. Turn left, then the second turn to the right. The Mad Lobster is opposite the church.

Séan: **Go raibh míle maith agat.**
Thanks very much.

Máire: **Tá fáilte romhat. Bain taitneamh as do bhéile!**
You're welcome. Enjoy your meal!

## VOCABULARY

| | |
|---|---|
| **An tIarthar** | the West |
| **thiar** | (in the) west |
| **ag dul siar** | going west |
| **ag teacht aniar** | coming from the west |
| | |
| **An Tuaisceart** | the North |
| **thuaidh** | (in the) north |
| **ag dul ó thuaidh** | going north |
| **ag teacht aduaidh** | coming from the north |
| **an ghaoth aduaidh** | the north wind |
| | |
| **An Deisceart** | the South |
| **theas** | (in the) south |
| **ag dul ó dheas** | going south |
| **ag teacht aneas** | coming from the south |

| **An tOirthear** | the East |
| **thoir** | (in the) east |
| **ag dul soir** | going east |
| **ag teacht anoir** | coming from the east |

A common expression in Connemara Irish is **Chuirfeadh sé soir thú!** "He'd drive you east," i.e. he'd drive you mad! (someone traveled east to Ballinasloe, the nearest asylum!)

At a musical session in a Gaeltacht pub, you will hear scores of these expressions:

| **Nár laga Dia thú!** | May God not weaken you! |
| **Ardfhear!** | Good man! |
| **An-bhean!** | Good woman! |
| **Dia go deo leat!** | God be with you forever! |
| **Mo ghrá do sciúch!** | Bless your voice! |

And as the music dies down—if it ever does—and people get immersed in the mysterious rituals of imbibing and conversing, many toasts and blessings will be heard:

| **Slainte mhaith!** | Good health! |
| **Gob fliuch agus bás in Éirinn!** | A wet mouth (beak) and death in Ireland! |
| **Sláinte an bhradáin chugat!** | The health of the salmon to you! |

And if you keep your ears open, you'll hear many such more, some of which you'd rather not repeat to your mother-in-law. There are also some bogus or botched blessings in English, purporting to come from the Irish. Beware of these ...

## GRAMMAR

### *Adverbs of Direction*

**amach** — "out" with a sense of motion.
**amuigh** — "out" or "outside" without the sense of motion, for example:

| **Chuaigh mé amach aréir.** | I went out last night. |
| **Tá duine éigin amuigh.** | Somebody is outside. |

**isteach** — "in" or "inside" with a sense of motion.
**istigh** — "in" or "inside" without a sense of motion, for example:

| | |
|---|---|
| **Tháinig frog isteach sa chistin.** | A frog came into the kitchen. |
| **An bhfuil éinne istigh?** | Is there anybody in? |

### More Verbs

Present

| **sábhálaim (sábháil)** save | | **tíolacaim (tíolaic)** accompany | |
|---|---|---|---|
| *Sing.* | *Pl.* | *Sing.* | *Pl.* |
| 1. sábhálaim | sábhálaimid | tíolacaim | tíolacaimid |
| 2. sábhálann tú | sábhálann sibh | tíolacann tú | tíolacann sibh |
| 3. sábhálann sé | sábhálann siad | tíolacann sé | tíolacann siad |
| *Autonomous* | | *Autonomous* | |
| sábháiltear | | tíolactar | |

Past Tense

| **sábhálaim (sábháil)** save | | **tíolacaim (tíolaic)** accompany | |
|---|---|---|---|
| *Sing.* | *Pl.* | *Sing.* | *Pl.* |
| 1. shábháil mé | shábhálamar | thíolaic mé | thíolacamar |
| 2. shábháil tú | shábháil sibh | thíolaic tú | thíolaic sibh |
| 3. shábháil sé | shábháil siad | thíolaic sé | thíolaic siad |
| *Autonomous* | | *Autonomous* | |
| sábháladh | | tíolacadh | |

## Past Habitual

| sábhálaim (sábháil) save | | tíolacaim (tíolaic) accompany | |
|---|---|---|---|
| *Sing.* | *Pl.* | *Sing.* | *Pl.* |
| 1. shábhálainn | shábhálaimis | thíolacainn | thíolacaimis |
| 2. shábháilteá | shábháladh sibh | thíolactá | thíolacadh sibh |
| 3. shábháladh sé | shábhálaidís | thíolacadh sé | thíolacaidís |
| *Autonomous* | | *Autonomous* | |
| shábháiltí | | thíolactaí | |

## Future

| sábhálaim (sábháil) save | | tíolacaim (tíolaic) accompany | |
|---|---|---|---|
| *Sing.* | *Pl.* | *Sing.* | *Pl.* |
| 1. sábhálfaidh mé | sábhálfaimid | tíolacfaidh mé | tíolacfaimid |
| 2. sábhálfaidh tú | sábhálfaidh sibh | tíolacfaidh tú | tíolfaidh sibh |
| 3. sábhálfaidh sé | sábhálfaidh siad | tíolacfaidh sé | tíolacfaidh siad |
| *Autonomous* | | *Autonomous* | |
| sábhálfar | | tíolacfar | |

## Conditional

| sábhálaim (sábháil) save | | tíolacaim (tíolaic) accompany | |
|---|---|---|---|
| *Sing.* | *Pl.* | *Sing.* | *Pl.* |
| 1. shábhálfainn | shábhálfaimis | thíolacfainn | thíolacfaimis |
| 2. shábhálfá | shábhálfadh sibh | thíolacfá | thíolacfadh sibh |
| 3. shábhálfadh sé | shábhálfaidís | thíolacfadh sé | thíolacfaidís |
| *Autonomous* | | *Autonomous* | |
| shábhálfaí | | thíolacfaí | |

Present Subjunctive

| sábhálaim (sábháil) save | | tíolacaim (tíolaic) accompany | |
|---|---|---|---|
| *Sing.* | *Pl.* | *Sing.* | *Pl.* |
| 1. sábhála mé | sábhálaimid | tíolaca mé | tíolacaimid |
| 2. sábhála tú | sábhála sibh | tíolaca tú | tíolaca sibh |
| 3. sábhála sé | sábhála siad | tíolaca sé | tíolaca siad |
| *Autonomous* | | *Autonomous* | |
| sábháiltear | | tíolactar | |

Imperative

| sábhálaim (sábháil) save | | tíolacaim (tíolaic) accompany | |
|---|---|---|---|
| *Sing.* | *Pl.* | *Sing.* | *Pl.* |
| 1. sábhálaim | sábhálaimis | tíolacaim | tíolacaimis |
| 2. sábháil | sábhálaigí | tíolaic | tíolacaigí |
| 3. sábháladh sé | sábhálaidís | tíolacadh sé | tíolacaidís |
| *Autonomous* | | *Autonomous* | |
| sábháiltear | | tíolactar | |

Verbal Noun

| sábhálaim (sábháil) save | tíolacaim (tíolaic) accompany |
|---|---|
| sábháil | tíolacadh |

Verbal Adjective

| sábhálaim (sábháil) save | tíolacaim (tíolaic) accompany |
|---|---|
| sábháilte | tíolactha |

**EXERCISE**

I saved the hay. **Shábháil mé an féar.**
How would you say: "Let us save the hay!"
Go to the Imperative (above) and the first person plural:
**Sábhálaimis an féar!**

God saved us. **Shábháil Dia sinn.**
How would you say: "May God save us!"
Go to the Present Subjunctive, third person singular:
**Go sábhála Dia sinn!**

## Irregular Verbs

The Irish language has ten irregular verbs. Verbs are identified by either the first person singular, the present indicative or by the second person singular imperative (in brackets). Only irregular parts of the verbs are indicated.

1. **beirim (beir)**                        I carry/catch/am born
   Past                                     rug mé, etc.
   Conditional                              bhéarfainn, etc.
   Verbal noun                              breith
   Verbal adjective                         beirthe

2. **cluinim (cluin)/cloisim (clois)**      I hear
   Past                                     chuala mé, etc.
   Past autonomous                          chualathas
   Verbal noun                              cluinstin/cloisteáil

3. **déanaim (déan)**                       I make
   Past (independent)                       rinne mé, etc/dhein mé, etc.
   Past (dependent)                         ní dhearna mé, etc.
   Verbal noun                              déanamh

4. **abraim/deirim (abair)**                I say
   Present                                  deirim, etc.
   Present habitual                         deirinn, etc.
   Present subjunctive                      go ndeire mé, etc.

| | |
|---|---|
| Past | dúirt mé, etc. |
| 1st pl. | dúramar |
| Past autonomous | dúradh |
| Future | déarfaidh mé, etc. |
| Conditional | déarfainn, etc. |
| Imperative | abraím, etc. |
| 2nd sing. | abair |
| Verbal noun | rá |
| Verbal adjective | ráite |

5. **faighim (faigh)** — I get

| | |
|---|---|
| Past | fuair mé, etc. |
| Past autonomous | fuarthas |
| Past (independent) | gheobhainn, etc. |
| 2nd sing. | gheofá |
| Past autonomous | gheofaí |
| Future (independent) | gheobhaidh mé, etc. |
| Future autonomous | gheofar |
| Future (dependent) | ní bhfaighidh mé, etc. |
| Future autonomous | ní bhfaighfear |
| Conditional (dependent) | ní bhfaighinn, etc. |
| 2nd sing. | ní bhfaighfeá |
| Conditional autonomous | ní bhfaighfí |
| Verbal noun | fáil |
| Verbal adjective | faighte |

6. **feicim (feic)** — I see

| | |
|---|---|
| Past (independent) | chonaic mé, etc. |
| Past autonomous | chonacthas |
| Past (dependent) | ní fhaca mé, etc. |
| Past autonomous | ní fhacthas |
| Verbal noun | feiceáil |
| Verbal adjective | feicthe |

7. **tagaim (tar)** — I come

| | |
|---|---|
| Present | tagaim, etc. |
| Present subjunctive | go dtaga mé, etc. |
| Past | tháinig mé, etc. |
| 1st pl. | thángamar |
| Past autonomous | thángthas |

| | |
|---|---|
| Past habitual | thagainn, etc. |
| Future | tiocfaidh mé, etc. |
| Conditional | thiocfainn, etc. |
| Imperative | tagaim, etc. |
| $2^{nd}$ sing. | tar |
| Verbal noun | teacht |
| Verbal adjective | tagtha |

**8. ithim (ith)**     I eat

| | |
|---|---|
| Future | íosfaidh mé, etc. |
| Conditional | d'íosfainn, etc. |
| Verbal noun | ithe |
| Verbal adjective | ite |

**9. téim (téigh)**     I go

| | |
|---|---|
| Past (dependent) | ní dheachaigh mé, etc. |
| $1^{st}$ pl. | ní dheachamar |
| Past (independent) | chuaigh mé, etc. |
| Past autonomous | chuathas |
| Past autonomous | ní dheachthas |
| Future | rachaidh mé, etc. |
| Future autonomous | rachfar |
| Conditional | rachainn, etc. |
| $2^{nd}$ sing. | rachfá |
| Conditional autonomous | rachfaí |
| Verbal noun | dul |
| Verbal adjective | dulta |

**10. tugaim (thug)**     I give

| | |
|---|---|
| Present | tugaim, etc. |
| Present subjunctive | go dtuga mé, etc. |
| Past | thug mé, etc. |
| Future | tabharfaidh mé, etc. |
| Conditional | thabharfainn, etc. |
| Past habitual | thugainn, etc. |
| Imperative | tugaim, etc. |
| $2^{nd}$ sing. | tabhair |
| Verbal noun | tabhairt |
| Verbal adjective | tugtha |

## The Verb "to be"

**táim (bí)**                              to be

| Present | | | |
|---|---|---|---|
| *Independent (Positive)* | | *Dependent (Negative)* | |
| 1. táim (tá mé) | táimid | nílim (níl mé) | nílimid |
| 2. tá tú | tá sibh | níl tú | níl sibh |
| 3. tá sé | tá siad | níl sé | níl siad |
| *Autonomous* | | go, etc., bhfuilim (bhfuil me, etc.) | |
| táthar | | níltear, go, etc., bhfuiltear | |

| Present Habitual | | Past Habitual | |
|---|---|---|---|
| 1. bím | bímid | bhínn | bhímis |
| 2. bíonn tú | bíonn sibh | bhíteá | bhíodh sibh |
| 3. bíonn sé | bíonn siad | bhíodh sé | bhídís |
| *Autonomous* | | | |
| bítear | | bhítí | |

| Past | | | |
|---|---|---|---|
| *Independent* | | *Dependent* | |
| 1. bhí mé | bhíomar | raibh mé | rabhamar |
| 2. bhí tú | bhí sibh | raibh tú | raibh sibh |
| 3. bhí sé | bhí siad | raibh sé | raibh siad |
| *Autonomous* | | | |
| bhíothas | | rabhthas | |

| Future | | Conditional and Past Subjunctive | |
|---|---|---|---|
| 1. beidh mé | beimid | bheinn | bheimis |
| 2. beidh tú | beidh sibh | bheifeá | bheadh sibh |
| 3. beidh sé | beidh siad | bheadh sé | bheidís |
| *Autonomous* | | | |
| beifear | | bheifí | |

| Present Subjunctive | | Imperative | |
|---|---|---|---|
| 1. raibh mé* | rabhaimid | bím | bímis |
| 2. raibh tú | raibh sibh | bí | bígí |
| 3. raibh sé | raibh siad | bíodh sé | bídís |
| *Autonomous* | | | |
| rabhthar | | bítear | |

*cha raibh mé (Ulster)

*Examples*
**Tá mé ag súil leat.**          I am expecting you.
**Bhí mé ag súil leat.**         I was expecting you.

Autonomous form:
**Táthar ag súil leat.**         You are expected.

**EXERCISE**

How would you say:
You are not expected.          **Níltear ag súil leat.**
You were expected.            **Bhíothas ag súil leat.**

# Lesson 6: In the Restaurant

Seosamh: **An bhfuil ocras ort, a chroí?**
Are you hungry, dear?

Laoise: **Ar m'anam, tá!**
I sure am!

Seosamh: **Cad déarfá leis an manglam cloicheán?**
What would you say to the prawn cocktail?

Laoise: **Ní déarfainn faic leis! Ding de mhealbhacán a bheidh agamsa!**
I'd say nothing to it! I'll have the wedge of melon!

Seosamh: **Agus ina dhiaidh sin?**
And after that?

Laoise: **Beidh an t-uibheagán beacán agam, is dóigh liom.**
I'll have the mushroom omelet I think.

Seosamh: **An mbeidh do dhóthain ansin agat?**
Will you have enough in that?

Laoise: **Beidh cinnte.**
I will to be sure.

Seosamh: **An stobhach gaelach a bheidh agamsa ... ní hea, b'fhearr liom turcaí stuáilte rósta agus liamhás.**
I'll have the Irish stew ... no, I'd prefer the roast stuffed turkey and ham.

Séan: **Cad a bheidh agat?**
What will you have?

Seosamh: **Beidh pionta agam.**
I'll have a pint.

Séan: **Beidh pionta agamsa freisin!**
I'll have a pint too!

Seosamh: **Pióg úll agus uachtar a bheidh agamsa. Cad fút féin?**
I'll have the apple pie and cream. What about yourself?

Laoise:     **Níl a fhios agam. Mionbhruar biabhóige agus uachtar reoite b'fhéidir.**
            I don't know. Rhubarb crumble and ice cream maybe.
Seosamh:    **Purgóid na manach a thugtaí ar an mbiabhóg fadó!**
            Long ago rhubarb was called the monks' purgative!


## VOCABULARY

We say of someone who gobbles down his food **Thug sé slogadh na lachan dá chuid bia!** "He gave his food the swallowing of a duck."

**Go seinne sé siar ort!** This could be said to the same person, meaning "may it play music behind you," i.e. may you break wind.

**Níl sé thar mholadh beirte.** It leaves much to be desired. (Literally, it is not beyond the praise of two people.)

Do you have a reservation? **Ar chuir tú bord in áirithe?** (answer: **chuir/níor chuir**)

| | |
|---|---|
| ale | **leann** |
| aperitif | **greadóg** |
| apple tart | **toirtín úll** (**úll** apple; **úllord** orchard) |
| apricot | **aibreog** (*pl.* **aibreoga**) |
| artichoke | **bliosán** (*pl.* **bliosáin**) |
| asparagus | **lus súgach** |
| bacon | **bagún** |
| basil | **basal** |
| bay leaf | **duille labhrais** |
| beans | **pónairí** (*sing.* **pónaire**) |
| beef | **mairteoil** |
| beer | **beoir** |
| beetroot | **biatas** |
| biscuit | **briosca** (*pl.* **brioscaí**) |
| black pudding | **putóg dhubh/lúbán dubh** |
| blackberries | **sméara dubha** (Púca na Sméar was a mischievous pooka or sprite that excreted on berries, betoking the withering days of autumn.) |

| | |
|---|---|
| blancmange | **bánghlóthach** |
| blue cheese | **gormán** |
| blueberry | **fraochán** |
| boiled | **bruite/beirithe** |
| boiled egg | **ubh bhruite** |
| bowl | **babhla** |
| braised | **galstofa** (**gal** steam; **inneall gaile** steam engine) |
| brandy | **branda** |
| bread | **arán** (**Ár n-arán laethúil tabhair dúinn inniu** "Give us this day our daily bread." — notice what happened to **arán** after **ár** "our") |
| bread roll | **rolla aráin** |
| brown bread | **arán donn** |
| breakfast | **bricfeasta** |
| broccoli | **brocailí** |
| broiled | **gríosctha** |
| Brussels sprouts | **bachlóga bhruiséile** |
| butter | **im** (**cam an ime** buttercup) |
| butter knife/side knife | **scian ime** |
| cabbage | **cabáiste** |
| cakes | **cístí** (*sing.* **císte**) |
| canapé spread | **leathán canapé** |
| carrot | **cairéad** |
| carvery | **spólann** |
| cauliflower | **cóilis** |
| caviar | **caibheár** |
| celery | **soilire** |
| cereal | **gránach** |
| champagne | **seaimpéin** |
| cheddar | **céadar** |
| cheese | **cáis** |
| cheese knife | **scian cháise** |
| cheese spread | **leathán cáise** |
| cheesecake | **císte cáise** |
| chef | **príomhchócaire** (**príomh** as a prefix "chief, main, principal," for example **príomhfheidhmeannach** chief executive) |

| cherry | **silín** |
|---|---|
| chicken | **sicín/circeoil** |
| chicory | **siocaire** |
| chili | **cilí** |
| chips | **sceallóga** |
| chives | **síobhais** |
| chop | **gríscín** (*n.*) |
| chowder | **seabhdar** |
| cider | **ceirtlis** |
| cockles | **ruacain** (*sing.* **ruacan**) |
| cocktail | **manglam** |
| coconut | **cnó cócó** (*pl.* cnónna cócó) |
| cod | **trosc** (**ola ae troisc** cod-liver oil) |
| coffee | **caife** |
| coleslaw | **cálslá** |
| condiments | **tarsainn** |
| cook | **cócaire** (*see* chef above) |
| corn | **arbhar** |
| corn on the cob | **arbhar sa dias** |
| cornflakes | **calóga arbhair** |
| cottage cheese | **cáis bhaile/cáis tí** |
| cottage pie/shepherd's pie | **pióg an aoire** |
| course | **cúrsa** (*pl.* **cúrsaí**) |
| crab | **portán** (*pl.* **portáin**) |
| cranberries | **mónóga** (*sing.* **mónóg**) |
| cream cheese | **cáis uachtair** |
| cream | **uachtar** (**Uachtarán** president) |
| creamed potatoes | **prátaí coipthe** (**prátaí** in Munster, **fataí** in Connaught) |
| crepe | **pancóg** |
| cucumber | **cúcamar** (*pl.* **cúcamair**) |
| cup | **cupán** (*see* saucer) |
| curried eggs | **uibheacha curaithe** (**ubh** egg, **ubhchruthach** oval) |
| custard | **custard** |
| cutlery | **sceanra** |
| cutlet | **gearrthóg** (*pl.* **gearrthóga**) |
| Danish Blue | **gormán Danmhargach** |
| date | **dáta** (*pl.* **dátaí**) |

| | |
|---|---|
| dessert wine/sweet wine | **fíon milis** |
| dessert | **milseog (milis** sweet, *adj.*) |
| digestive biscuit | **briosca díleách** |
| dill | **lus mín** |
| dinner | **dinnéar** |
| dish | **mias** |
| doughnut | **taoschnó (cnó** nut; notice lenition — cnó/taoschnó) |
| draught beer | **beoir bhairille** |
| dressing | **blastán** |
| drink | **deoch** |
| dry wine | **fíon géar** |
| duck | **lacha** ("quack quack" is "vác vác" in Irish) |
| dumplings | **dumplagáin** |
| eclair | **éadromóg** |
| eggs | **uibheacha (ubh** egg) |
| egg salad | **sailéad uibhe** |
| eggplant | **ubhthoradh (ubh** egg; **toradh** fruit) |
| fennel | **finéal** |
| fig | **fige** (*pl.* **figí**) |
| fillet | **filléad** |
| fillet steak | **stéig filléid** |
| fish | **iasc (iasc as uisce i do bhéal!** "A fish from water in your mouth!" An imprecation, meaning "Watch your language," said to someone using foul speech.) |
| fish fillet | **filléad éisc** |
| food | **bia** |
| fork | **forc/gabhlóg** |
| four course meal | **béile ceithre chúrsa** (note lenition following **ceithre** four) |
| French bean | **pónaire Fhrancach** (note feminine here and masculine next two entries) |
| French bread | **arán Francach** |
| French dressing | **blastán Francach** |
| French/pan fried | **friochta** |
| fried eggs | **uibheacha friochta** |

| | |
|---|---|
| fruit | **torthaí** (*sing.* **toradh**) |
| fruit juice | **sú torthaí** |
| fruit salad | **sailéad torthaí** |
| fruit tart | **toirtín torthaí** |
| garden peas | **piseanna garraí** |
| garlic | **gairleog** |
| garlic mushrooms | **beacáin ghairleoige/muisiriúin ghairleoige** (look at the **in** slender endings of the nouns **beacáin** and **muisiriúin** which soften the garlic with lenition) |
| gherkin | **gircín** |
| gin | **jin** |
| ginger (ale) | **uisce sinséir** (look at the slenderization of the ginger in the genitive — sinséar/sinséir) |
| ginger | **sinséar** |
| glass | **gloine** |
| gooseberries | **spíonáin** (*sing.* **spíonán**) |
| goulash | **gúlais** |
| grapefruit | **seadóg** (*pl.* **seadóga**) |
| grapes | **caora fíniúna** (*sing.* **caor finiúna**) |
| green bean | **pónaire ghlas** (notice the feminine adjective here, on the bean, and the masculine adjective on the pepper that follows) |
| green pepper | **piobar glas** |
| grilled | **griollta** |
| grilled salmon steak | **stéig ghriollta bradáin** |
| grilled t-bone steak | **stéig t-chnáimhe ghriollta** |
| haddock | **cadóg** |
| half-one (whiskey) | **leathghloine** (**gloine** softened by what comes before) |
| half-pint | **leathphionta** (**pionta** softened by the preceding) |
| halibut | **haileabó** |
| ham | **liamhás** |
| hamburger | **burgar** |
| hard-boiled egg | **ubh chruabhruite** |

| | |
|---|---|
| herbs | **luibheanna** (*sing.* **luibh**) |
| herring | **scadán** |
| honey | **mil** (Cluain Meala, the place name; **Clonmel** "meadow of honey") |
| hot chocolate | **seacláid the** (adjective softened for chocolate) |
| hot dog | **brocaire te** (adjective not softened) |
| hot whiskey | **fuisce te** (Another term for whiskey is **uisce beatha** "water of life," an example of an English word derived from Irish.) |
| hotel | **óstán/óstlann** |
| house wine | **fíon an tí** |
| ice cream | **uachtar reoite** |
| Irish blue (cheese) | **gormán Éireannach** |
| Irish coffee | **caife gaelach** |
| Irish dressing | **blastán Éireannach** |
| Irish stew | **stobhach gaelach** |
| jam | **subh** |
| jelly | **glóthach** |
| jug | **crúiscín** |
| kebab | **ceibeab** |
| ketchup | **citseap** |
| kidney beans | **pónáirí duánacha** |
| kippers | **scadáin leasaithe** (*sing.* **scadán leasaithe**) |
| knife | **scian** (*pl.* **sceana**) |
| lager | **lágar** |
| lamb | **uaineoil** |
| lasagna with side salad | **lasáinne agus sailéad taoibh** |
| leek | **cainneann** |
| lemon | **líomóid** (*pl.* **líomóidí**) |
| lemon (juice) | **sú líomóide** |
| lemon cheesecake | **císte cáise líomóide** |
| lemonade | **líomanáid** |
| lentil | **piseánach** |
| lettuce | **leitís** |
| lime | **líoma** |
| liqueur | **licéar** |

| | |
|---|---|
| liver | **ae** (**A chara na n-ae istigh!** "O friend of my inmost heart!" — In Irish physiology, the liver is no mean organ.) |
| lobster bisque | **bísc ghliomaigh** |
| lobster | **gliomach** |
| lounge | **tolglann** (**tolg** sofa. **-lann** is a common suffix: **leabharlann** library; **otharlann** infirmary; **bialann** restaurant) |
| lunch | **lón** |
| mackerel | **príomhchúrsa** (**cúrsa** softened by **príomh**) |
| mango | **mangó** |
| marmalade | **marmaláid** |
| marrow | **mearóg** |
| marshmallow | **leamhnachán** |
| mayonnaise | **maonáis** |
| meat | **feoil** |
| meat loaf | **builín feola** (note the genitive case ending) |
| meat patty | **pióigín feola** |
| meat pie | **pióg feola** |
| medium | **cnagbhruite** |
| melon fan | **fean mealbhacáin** |
| melon gondola | **naomhóg mhealbhacáin** (a **naomhóg** is a Kerry currach) |
| melon | **mealbhacán** |
| melon wedge | **ding de mhealbhacán** |
| menu | **biachlár** |
| meringue | **meireang** |
| milk | **bainne** |
| milkshake | **creathán bainne** |
| minced meat | **mionfheoil** |
| mineral (water) | **uisce mianraí** |
| minestrone | **mineastróine** |
| mint | **miontas** |
| mixed grill | **griolladh measctha** |
| monkfish | **anglait/bráthair** |
| muffin | **bocaire** |

| | |
|---|---|
| mulled wine | **scailtín fíona** |
| mushroom | **beacán/muisiriún** |
| mushroom omelet | **uibheagán beacán/uibheagán muisiriún** |
| mussels | **diúilicíní** |
| mustard | **mustard** |
| noodles | **núdail** |
| napkin | **naipcín** |
| nuts | **cnónna** (*sing.* **cnó**) |
| omelet | **uibheagán** |
| onion | **oinniúin** |
| onion ring | **fáinne oinniúin** |
| orange (juice) | **sú oráistí** |
| orange | **oráiste** |
| ox tongue | **damhtheanga** (**damh** ox + **teanga**, tongue/language, as in **Tír gan teanga tír gan anam** "A country without a language is a country without a soul.") |
| oysters | **oisrí** (*sing.* **oisre**) |
| pancake | **pancóg** (*pl.* **pancóga**) |
| pan fried/fried | **friochta** |
| parmesan | **parmasán** |
| parsley | **peirsil** |
| parsnip | **meacan bán** |
| pasta | **pasta** |
| peach | **péitseog** (*pl.* **péitseoga**) |
| pear | **piorra** (*pl.* **piorraí**) |
| peas | **piseanna** |
| pepper | **piobar** |
| pepper castor | **piobarán** |
| pheasant | **piasún** (*pl.* **piasúin**) |
| pie | **pióg** (*pl.* **píoga**) |
| pineapple | **anann** (*pl.* **anainn**) |
| pint | **pionta** |
| piquant herrings | **scadáin ghoinbhlasta** |
| plaice | **leathóg** |
| plate | **pláta** (*pl.* **plátaí**) |
| plum | **pluma** (*pl.* **plumaí**) |

| | |
|---|---|
| poached | **scalta** |
| poached egg | **ubh scalta** |
| pork | **muiceoil** (**muc** pig; **feoil** meat) |
| potato | **práta** |
| potato chips | **sceallóga prátaí** (*pl.* **prátaí**) |
| potato salad | **sailéad prátaí** |
| poultry | **circeoil** |
| prawn | **cloicheán** (*pl.* **cloicheáin**) |
| prawn cocktail | **manglam cloicheán** |
| pub grub | **bia tábhairne** |
| public house | **tábhairne/teach ósta** |
| pumpkin | **puimcín** (*pl.* **puimciní**) |
| quail | **gearg** |
| radish | **raidis** |
| rainbow trout | **breac dea-dhathach** |
| rare | **tearcbhruite** |
| rashers | **slisíní** |
| raspberries | **sútha craobh** (*sing.* **sú craobh**) |
| red cabbage | **cabáiste dearg** |
| red cheddar | **céadar rua** |
| red currants | **cuiríní dearga** |
| red pepper | **piobar dearg** |
| red wine | **fíon dearg** |
| reservation | **áirithint** |
| restaurant | **bialann** (*pl.* **bialanna**) |
| rhubarb | **biabhóg** |
| rhubarb crumble and custard · | **mionbhruar biabhóige agus custard** |
| rib roast | **spóla easnacha** |
| rice | **rís** |
| rice crispies | **brioscáin ríse** |
| roast potatoes | **prátaí rósta** |
| roast rib of beef with<br>  horseradish sauce | **easna rósta mairteola le hanlann**<br>  **raidise fiáine** (**fiáin** is "wild";<br>  **fiáine** is the genitive form fol-<br>  lowing a feminine noun) |
| roast stuffed chicken and ham | **sicín stuáilte rósta agus liamhás** |
| roast turkey | **turcaí rósta** |
| roasted | **rósta** |
| rolled brisket | **briscéad rollta** |

| | |
|---|---|
| rosemary | **marós** |
| round steak | **stéig chruinn** (**cruinn** round; **an chruinne** the universe, the world) |
| runner-bean | **pónaire reatha** |
| Russian salad | **sailéad rúiseach** |
| salad | **sailéad** (*pl.* **sailéid**) |
| salad cream | **uachtar sailéid** |
| salami | **salami** |
| salmon | **bradán** (in Old Irish the word was **eo**, the root of **eolas** "knowledge," **eochair** "a key," **eolaíocht** "science") |
| salt | **salann** |
| saltcellar | **sáiltéar** |
| sandwiches | **ceapairí** (*sing.* **ceapaire**) |
| sardines | **sairdíní** |
| sauce | **anlann** (Proverb: **Is maith an t-anlann an t-ocras** "Hunger is a good sauce." Notice how **anlann** and **ocras** are masculine nouns. The nominative form, following the article, is **an t-anlann, an t-ocras**.) |
| saucer | **fochupán** (**cupán** a cup. **Fo-** is a prefix denoting "under" or "secondary": **fobhealach** subway (fo + bealach), **fochiall** secondary meaning (fo + ciall) and so on.) |
| sausage | **ispín** |
| sautéed | **sótáilte** |
| savory omelet | **uibheagán neamh-mhilis** (**milis** sweet, **neamh-** is a prefix denoting "non": **neamhchúthail** unbashful (neamh + cuthail); **cúthail** = bashful; **neamhdhíobhálach** = harmless (neamh + díobhálach). |
| savoy cabbage | **cabáiste saváí** |
| scone | **scóna** |
| Scotch egg | **ubh Albanach** |
| scrambled egg | **ubh scrofa** |
| sea trout | **breac geal** |

| | |
|---|---|
| seafood | **bia mara** (*sing.* **muir — Ar muir is ar tír** "on sea and on land") |
| selection of cold meat platters | **rogha de thrinsiúir feolta fuara** |
| selection of cold meat salads | **rogha de shailéid feolta fuara** |
| self-service | **féinseirbhís** (The prefix **féin-** does not soften **seirbhís** — in compound nouns *s* is not softened after *n*.) |
| service charge | **táille sheirbhíse** |
| service charge not included | **níl seirbhís san áireamh** |
| shellfish | **éisc shliogánacha** |
| shepherd's pie/cottage pie | **píóg an aoire** |
| sherry | **seiris** |
| shish kebab | **ceibeab** |
| side knife/butter knife | **scian ime** |
| silver side of beef | **íostiarpa mairteola** |
| sirloin of beef with horseradish sauce | **caoldroim rósta mairteola le hanlann raidise fiáine** |
| sirloin steak | **stéig chaoldroma** |
| small fork | **forc beag** |
| smoked salmon | **bradán deataithe** |
| soda (water) | **uisce sóide** |
| soft-boiled egg | **ubh bhogbhruite** |
| sole | **sól** |
| sherbet | **soirbéad** |
| soufflé | **cúróg** |
| soup | **anraith** |
| soup spoon | **spúnóg anraith** |
| spaghetti | **spaigití** |
| spaghetti bolognese | **spaigití bologna** |
| spareribs | **lomeasnacha** |
| spinach | **spionáiste** |
| sponge cake | **císte spúinse** |
| spoon | **spúnóg** (*pl.* **spúnóga**) |
| spring onion | **oinniún earraigh** (**earrach** spring — note the genitive of this masculine noun) |
| starter | **cúrsa tosaigh** |
| steak | **stéig** (note the genitive of this feminine noun in the following entry) |

| | |
|---|---|
| steak knife | **scian stéige** |
| steamed | **galaithe** |
| stew | **stobhach** |
| stewed | **stofa** |
| stewing steak | **stéig stobhaidh** |
| stout | **leann dubh** |
| strawberries | **sútha talún** (**talún** is a genitive for **talamh**, earth, ground, land) |
| stuffing | **búiste** |
| sugar | **siúcra** |
| sundae | **sundae** |
| supper | **suipéar** |
| sweet corn | **arbhar milis** |
| sweet wine/dessert wine | **fíon milis** |
| sweets | **milseáin** (*sing.* **milseán**) |
| Swiss cheese | **cáis Eilvéiseach** |
| table | **bord** (**tábla** in Ulster Irish) |
| table for two (three/four) | **bord do bheirt (thriúr/cheathrar)** |
| table service | **seirbhís ag an mbord** |
| tablecloth | **éadach boird** |
| tableware | **gréithe** |
| tangerine | **táinséirín** |
| tarragon | **dragan** |
| t-bone steak | **stéig t-chnáimhe** |
| tea | **tae** |
| teapot | **taephota** |
| teaspoon | **taespúnóg** |
| thyme | **tím** |
| tip | **aisce** |
| toast | **tósta** |
| tomato | **tráta** |
| tomato ketchup | **citseap trátaí** |
| tomato salad | **sailéad trátaí** |
| trifle | **traidhfil** |
| trimmings | **séasúr** |
| trout | **breac** (**breac** as an adjective is speckled) |
| truffle | **strufal** |
| tuna | **tuinnín** |

| | |
|---|---|
| turkey | **turcaí** |
| turnip | **turnapa** (*pl.* **turnapaí**) |
| vanilla | **fanaile** |
| veal | **laofheoil** |
| vegetables | **glasraí** |
| vegetarian | **feoilséantach** *adj.*; **feoilséantóir** *n.* |
| vinaigrette | **fínéigréad** |
| vinegar | **fínéagar** |
| vodka | **vadca** |
| waiter | **freastalaí** |
| waiter service | **seirbhís ag an mbord** |
| waitress | **banfhreastalaí** (Prefix **ban** denotes female; **altra** a nurse, **banaltra** female nurse) |
| watermelon | **mealbhacán uisce** |
| well-done | **lánbhruite** |
| Wexford (cheese) | **carmán** |
| whiskey | **uisce beatha/fuisce** |
| white bread | **arán bán** |
| white pudding | **putóg bhán/lúbán bán** |
| white wine | **fíon geal** |
| whiting | **faoitín** |
| wine | **fíon** |
| wine glass | **gloine fíona** |
| wine list | **clár an fhíona** |
| wine waiter/waitress | **fear/bean an fhíona** |
| yogurt | **iógart** |
| zucchini | **cúirséad** |

## GRAMMAR

### Noun-centering

One could say that Irish is a noun-centered language. To ask "Are you hungry?" in Irish, you would say **An bhfuil ocras ort**, literally: Is there hunger on you? The noun **ocras** is used here in preference to the adjective **ocrach**. These are perfectly natural in Irish. It's only when the sentences are translated into another language (and another culture) that they may sound quaint, or odd. The conventions and the mindset of one language can never be used to evaluate another.

Further examples:

| | |
|---|---|
| **Tá tart orm.** | I am thirsty. |
| **Ta fuacht orm.** | I am cold. |
| **Tá tuirse orm.** | I am tired. |
| **Tá olc uirthi.** | She is angry. |

### The Verb "mol"

Seosamh said **Cad déarfá?** "What would you say?" He could have said: **Cad a mholfá?** "What would you recommend?" The answer would be **Mholfainn ...** "I would recommend ..."

A proverb says: **Mol an óige agus tiocfaidh sí** Praise youth and it will flourish.

Let's look at the verb **mol**, expressing praise or recommendation, in the present tense.

| | |
|---|---|
| **molaim** | I praise |
| **molann tú** | you praise |
| **molann sé** | he praises |
| **molann sí** | she praises |
| **molaimid** | we praise |
| **molann sibh** | you (*pl.*) praise |
| **molann siad** | they praise |
| **moltar** | it is praised |

We lenite or soften the **m** in the past tense. **Mhol sé an bheoir**. He praised the beer.

Future Tense
An example of the future tense:
**Molfaidh mé an Tiarna.**          I will praise the Lord.

Conditional Tense
An example of the conditional:

**An molfá dom é a léamh?**          Would you recommend me to read it?
**Mholfainn!**                       I would!


*The Suffix "sa"*

The suffix **sa** in **agamsa** is a slight emphasis:

**An stobhach gaelach a**          I'll have the Irish stew.
  **bheidh agamsa.**

*Negation*

To form a negative answer, use **ní** and lenition:
**Ní thiocfaidh**
**Ní bhuailfidh**
**Ní thosóidh**


*The Word "faoi"*

The word **faoi** has many uses in Irish. One of its uses is the following:
*Cad tá fúm a dhéanamh?*          *What do I intend to do?*

**Cad tá fút a dhéanamh?**          What do you intend to do?
**Cad ta fúithi a dhéanamh?**       What does she intend to do?
**Cad tá faoi a dhéanamh?**         What does he intend to do?
**Cad tá fúinn a dhéanamh?**        What do we intend to do?
**Cad tá fuibh a dhéanamh?**        What do you (*pl.*) intend to do?
**Cad tá fúthu a dhéanamh?**        What do they intend to do?
**Cad fút féin?**                   What about yourself?


*The Verb "to know"*

**Níl a fhios agam.**               I don't know.
**Níl a fhios agat.**               You don't know.
**Níl a fhios aici.**               She does not know.

| | |
|---|---|
| **Níl a fhios aige.** | He doesn't know. |
| **Níl a fhios againn.** | We do not know. |
| **Níl a fhios agaibh.** | You (*pl.*) do not know. |
| **Níl a fhios acu.** | They do not know. |

## Interrogative

As a general rule we use **fios** for a thing, **aithne** for a person and **eolas** for a place.

| | |
|---|---|
| **An bhfuil a fhios agat?** | Do you know? |
| **An bhfuil aithne agat ar Sheosamh?** | Do you know Joseph? |
| **Tá seanaithne agam air. Is pleidhce é.** | I know him well. He's a fool. |
| **Níl eolas ar bith agam ar Chorcaigh.** | I don't know Cork at all. |

## Defective Verbs

**Feadair** is a Munsterism, a defective verb:
**Ní fheadair sé inniu ó inné.** He doesn't know today from yesterday (somebody that's mixed up).

## More Verbs

Present

| **cráim (cráigh)** I torment | | **dóim (dóigh)** I burn | |
|---|---|---|---|
| *Sing.* | *Pl.* | *Sing.* | *Pl.* |
| 1. cráim | cráimid | dóim | dóimid |
| 2. cránn tú | cránn sibh | dónn tú | dónn sibh |
| 3. cránn sé | cránn siad | dónn sé | dónn siad |
| *Autonomous* | | *Autonomous* | |
| cráitear | | dóitear | |

Past Tense

| cráim (cráigh) I torment | | dóim (dóigh) I burn | |
|---|---|---|---|
| *Sing.* | *Pl.* | *Sing.* | *Pl.* |
| 1. chráigh mé | chrámar | dhóigh mé | dhómar |
| 2. chráigh tú | chráigh sibh | dhóigh tú | dhóigh sibh |
| 3. chráigh sé | chráigh siad | dhóigh sé | dhóigh siad |
| *Autonomous* | | *Autonomous* | |
| crádh | | dódh | |

Past Habitual

| cráim (cráigh) I torment | | dóim (dóigh) I burn | |
|---|---|---|---|
| *Sing.* | *Pl.* | *Sing.* | *Pl.* |
| 1. chráinn | chráimis | dhóinn | dhóimis |
| 2. chráiteá | chrádh sibh | dhóiteá | dhódh sibh |
| 3. chrádh sé | chráidís | dhódh sé | dhóidís |
| *Autonomous* | | *Autonomous* | |
| chráití | | dhóití | |

Future

| cráim (cráigh) I torment | | dóim (dóigh) I burn | |
|---|---|---|---|
| *Sing.* | *Pl.* | *Sing.* | *Pl.* |
| 1. cráfaidh mé | cráfaimid | dófaidh mé | dófaimid |
| 2. cráfaidh tú | cráfaidh sibh | dófaidh tú | dófaidh sibh |
| 3. cráfaidh sé | cráfaidh siad | dófaidh sé | dófaidh siad |
| *Autonomous* | | *Autonomous* | |
| cráfar | | dófar | |

## Conditional

| cráim (cráigh) I torment | | dóim (dóigh) I burn | |
|---|---|---|---|
| *Sing.* | *Pl.* | *Sing.* | *Pl.* |
| 1. chráfainn | chráfaimis | dhófainn | dhófaimis |
| 2. chráfá | chráfadh sibh | dhófá | dhófadh sibh |
| 3. chráfadh sé | chráfaidís | dhófadh sé | dhófaidís |
| *Autonomous* | | *Autonomous* | |
| chráfaí | | dhófaí | |

## Present Subjunctive

| cráim (cráigh) I torment | | dóim (dóigh) I burn | |
|---|---|---|---|
| *Sing.* | *Pl.* | *Sing.* | *Pl.* |
| 1. crá mé | cráimid | dó mé | dóimid |
| 2. crá tú | crá sibh | dó tú | dó sibh |
| 3. crá sé | crá siad | dó sé | dó siad |
| *Autonomous* | | *Autonomous* | |
| cráitear | | dóitear | |

## Imperative

| cráim (cráigh) I torment | | dóim (dóigh) I burn | |
|---|---|---|---|
| *Sing.* | *Pl.* | *Sing.* | *Pl.* |
| 1. cráim | cráimis | dóim | dóimis |
| 2. cráigh | cráigí | dóigh | dóigí |
| 3. crádh sé | cráidís | dódh sé | dóidís |
| *Autonomous* | | *Autonomous* | |
| cráitear | | dóitear | |

Verbal Noun

| cráim (cráigh) I torment | dóim (dóigh) I burn |
|:---:|:---:|
| crá | dó |

Verbal Adjective

| cráim (cráigh) I torment | dóim (dóigh) I burn |
|:---:|:---:|
| cráite | dóite |

**EXERCISE**

I burned my hand. **Dhóigh mé mo lámh.**
*How would you say: "My hand was burned"?*

Go to the Past tense (above) and to the autonomous form: **Dódh mo lámh.**

Now, supposing some poor unfortunate had the habit of burning his hand every day. How would you say, "He used to burn his hand every day"? This is not exactly the Past; it wasn't one particular event in the past. Go, instead, to the Past Habitual, third person singular: **Dhódh sé a lámh gach lá.**

# Lesson 7: Time and Date

Seosamh: **Cathain a fheicfidh mé arís tú, a thaisce?**
When will I see you again, my treasure?

Laoise: **Ag Dia amháin atá a fhios ...**
Only God knows.

Seosamh: **Dé Luain?**
Monday?

Laoise: **Tá coinne agam leis an bhfiaclóir, is oth liom a rá.**
I have an appointment with the dentist, I regret to say.

Seosamh: **Dé Máirt mar sin?**
Tuesday so?

Laoise: **Beidh aintín liom ag teacht ar cuairt.**
I have an aunt coming to visit me.

Seosamh: **Dé Céadaoin?**
Wednesday?

Laoise: **Rang Ióga.**
Yoga class.

Seosamh: **Déardaoin?**
Thursday?

Laoise: **Rang Cócaireachta ...**
Cookery class ...

Seosamh: **Dé hAoine?**
Friday?

Laoise: **Beidh orm m'aintín a thabhairt go dtí an stáisiún.**
I'll have to bring my aunt to the station.

Seosamh: **Cad mar gheall ar an Satharn?**
What about Saturday?

Laoise: **Dé Sathairn ... sea, cuir glao orm ar an Satharn, nó ar an Domhnach.**
Saturday ... yes, call me on Saturday, or on Sunday.

## VOCABULARY

To this day in Irish-speaking Ireland, parts of the year are often associated with national or local feast days:

| | |
|---|---|
| **Lá Fhéile Bríde** | St Brigid's Day |
| **Lá Fhéile Pádraig** | St Patrick's Day |
| **Oíche Fhéile Eoin** | St John's Eve |
| **Oíche Shamhna** | Halloween |
| **Lá an Dreoilín** | Wran (wren) Day, St Stephen's Day |

| | |
|---|---|
| from day to day | **ó lá go lá** |
| often | **go minic** |
| very often | **go mion minic** |
| yesterday | **inné** |
| tomorrow | **amárach** |
| soon | **ar ball** |
| a while ago | **ó chianaibh** |
| the whole time | **an t-am ar fad** |
| in due time | **in am tráth** |
| tomorrow evening | **tráthnóna amárach** |
| tonight | **anocht** |
| tomorrow night | **istoíche amárach** |
| rush hour | **broidtráth** |
| next week | **an tseachtain seo chugainn** |
| next year | **an bhliain seo chugainn** |
| last year | **arú anuraidh** |
| the day after tomorrow | **amanathar** |
| now | **anois** |
| long ago | **fadó** |
| to the end of time | **go deo** (forever) |
| weekly | **in aghaidh na seachtaine** |
| a week ago | **seachtain ó shin** |
| a fortnight ago | **coicís ó shin** |

| | |
|---|---|
| **An mbuailfidh tú liom amárach?** | Will you meet with me tomorrow? |
| **Buailfidh.** | I will (meet). |
| **An dtosóidh sé in am?** | Will it start on time? |
| **Tosóidh.** | It will. |

The months of the year:

| | |
|---|---|
| January | **Eanáir** |
| February | **Feabhra** |
| March | **Márta** |
| April | **Aibreán** |
| May | **Bealtaine** |
| June | **Meitheamh** |
| July | **Iúil** |
| August | **Lúnasa** |
| September | **Meán Fómhair** |
| October | **Deireadh Fómhair** |
| November | **Samhain** |
| December | **Nollaig** |

Usually, in a conversation, we use the word **mí** "month":

| | |
|---|---|
| **mí an Mhárta** | the month of March |
| **mí na Samhna** | the month of November, etc. |

## GRAMMAR

*The imperative mood — 2ⁿᵈ person sing.*

| | |
|---|---|
| **Dún an doras.** | Close the door. |
| **Oscail an fhuinneog**. | Open the window. |

To form the negative, start with **ná** and put an **h** before the vowel, if there is one:

| | |
|---|---|
| **Ná dún an doras.** | Do not close the door. |
| **Ná hoscail an fhuinneog.** | Do not open the window. |

In the plural:

| | |
|---|---|
| **Ná dúnaigí an doras.** | Do not close the door. |
| **Ná hosclaígí an fhuinneog.** | Do not open the window. |

Because **dún** is one syllable the ending is **-aigí**. Because **oscail** is a two-syllable word, the ending is **-aígí**.

Look at the behavior of broad verbs such as **glan** (clean), **mol** (praise, recommend) and the slender verbs, **rith** (run), **buail** (hit) in the plural form of the imperative:
**glanaigí** (-aigí)
**molaigí** (-aigí)
**rithigí** (-igí)
**buailigí** (-igí)

Consult a grammar book for irregular forms such as **tabhair** (give) > **tugaigí** and **tar** (come) > **tagaigí**.

### More Verbs

Present

| léim (léigh) I read | | fím (figh) I weave | |
|---|---|---|---|
| *Sing.* | *Pl.* | *Sing.* | *Pl.* |
| 1. léim | léimid | fím | fímid |
| 2. léann tú | léann sibh | fíonn tú | fíonn sibh |
| 3. léann sé | léann siad | fíonn sé | fíonn siad |
| *Autonomous* | | *Autonomous* | |
| léitear | | fitear | |

Past Tense

| léim (léigh) I read | | fím (figh) I weave | |
|---|---|---|---|
| *Sing.* | *Pl.* | *Sing.* | *Pl.* |
| 1. léigh mé | léamar | d'fhigh mé | d'fhíomar |
| 2. léigh tú | léigh sibh | d'fhigh tú | d'fhigh sibh |
| 3. léigh sé | léigh siad | d'fhigh sé | d'fhigh siad |
| *Autonomous* | | *Autonomous* | |
| léadh | | fíodh | |

## Past Habitual

| léim (léigh) I read | | fím (figh) I weave | |
|---|---|---|---|
| *Sing.* | *Pl.* | *Sing.* | *Pl.* |
| 1. léinn | léimis | d'fhínn | d'fhímis |
| 2. léiteá | léadh sibh | d'fhíteá | d'fhíodh sibh |
| 3. léadh sé | léidís | d'fhíodh sé | d'fhídís |
| *Autonomous* | | *Autonomous* | |
| léití | | d'fhítí | |

## Future

| léim (léigh) I read | | fím (figh) I weave | |
|---|---|---|---|
| *Sing.* | *Pl.* | *Sing.* | *Pl.* |
| 1. léifidh mé | léifimid | fífidh mé | fífimid |
| 2. léifidh tú | léifidh sibh | fífidh tú | fífidh sibh |
| 3. léifidh sé | léifidh siad | fífidh sé | fífidh siad |
| *Autonomous* | | *Autonomous* | |
| léifear | | fífear | |

## Conditional

| léim (léigh) I read | | fím (figh) I weave | |
|---|---|---|---|
| *Sing.* | *Pl.* | *Sing.* | *Pl.* |
| 1. léifinn | léifimis | d'fhífinn | d'fhífimis |
| 2. léifeá | léifeadh sibh | d'fhífeá | d'fhífeadh sibh |
| 3. léifeadh sé | léifidís | d'fhífeadh sé | d'fhífidís |
| *Autonomous* | | *Autonomous* | |
| léifí | | d'fhífí | |

## Present Subjunctive

| léim (léigh) I read | | fím (figh) I weave | |
|---|---|---|---|
| *Sing.* | *Pl.* | *Sing.* | *Pl.* |
| 1. lé mé | léimid | fí mé | fímid |
| 2. lé tú | lé sibh | fí tú | fí sibh |
| 3. lé sé | lé siad | fí sé | fí siad |
| *Autonomous* | | *Autonomous* | |
| léitear | | fítear | |

## Imperative

| léim (léigh) I read | | fím (figh) I weave | |
|---|---|---|---|
| *Sing.* | *Pl.* | *Sing.* | *Pl.* |
| 1. léim | léimis | fím | fímis |
| 2. léigh | léigí | fígh | fígí |
| 3. léadh sé | léidís | fíodh sé | fídís |
| *Autonomous* | | *Autonomous* | |
| léitear | | fítear | |

## Verbal Noun

| léim (léigh) I read | fím (figh) I weave |
|---|---|
| léamh | fí |

## Verbal Adjective

| léim (léigh) I read | fím (figh) I weave |
|---|---|
| léite | fite |

**EXERCISE**

Collect your thoughts. **Cruinnigh do mheabhair.**

How would you say "Collect your thoughts" in the plural? Go to the Imperative, second person plural: **Cruinnígí bhur meabhair.**

Present Tense

| ceanglaím (ceangail) I tie | | díbrím (díbir) I banish | |
|---|---|---|---|
| *Sing.* | *Pl.* | *Sing.* | *Pl.* |
| 1. ceanglaím | ceanglaímid | díbrím | díbrímid |
| 2. ceanglaíonn tú | ceanglaíonn sibh | díbríonn tú | díbríonn sibh |
| 3. ceanglaíonn sé | ceanglaíonn siad | díbríonn sé | díbríonn siad |
| *Autonomous* | | *Autonomous* | |
| ceanglaítear | | díbrítear | |

Past Tense

| ceanglaím (ceangail) I tie | | díbrím (díbir) I banish | |
|---|---|---|---|
| *Sing.* | *Pl.* | *Sing.* | *Pl.* |
| 1. cheangail mé | cheanglaíomar | dhíbir mé | dhíbríomar |
| 2. cheangail tú | cheangail sibh | dhíbir tú | dhíbir sibh |
| 3. cheangail sé | cheangail siad | dhíbir sé | dhíbir siad |
| *Autonomous* | | *Autonomous* | |
| ceanglaíodh | | díbríodh | |

## Past Habitual

| ceanglaím (ceangail) I tie | | díbrím (díbir) I banish | |
|---|---|---|---|
| *Sing.* | *Pl.* | *Sing.* | *Pl.* |
| 1. cheanglaínn | cheanglaímis | dhíbrínn | dhíbrímis |
| 2. cheanglaíteá | cheanglaíodh sibh | dhíbríteá | dhíbríodh sibh |
| 3. cheanglaíodh sé | cheanglaídís | dhíbríodh sé | dhíbrídís |
| *Autonomous* | | *Autonomous* | |
| cheanglaítí | | dhíbrítí | |

## Future

| ceanglaím (ceangail) I tie | | díbrím (díbir) I banish | |
|---|---|---|---|
| *Sing.* | *Pl.* | *Sing.* | *Pl.* |
| 1. ceanglóidh mé | ceanglóimid | díbreoidh mé | díbreoimid |
| 2. ceanglóidh tú | ceanglóidh sibh | díbreoidh tú | díbreoidh sibh |
| 3. ceanglóidh sé | ceanglóidh siad | díbreoidh sé | díbreoidh siad |
| *Autonomous* | | *Autonomous* | |
| ceanglófar | | díbreofar | |

## Conditional

| ceanglaím (ceangail) I tie | | díbrím (díbir) I banish | |
|---|---|---|---|
| *Sing.* | *Pl.* | *Sing.* | *Pl.* |
| 1. cheanglóinn | cheanglóimis | dhíbreoinn | dhíbreoimis |
| 2. cheanglófá | cheanglódh sibh | dhíbreofá | dhíbreodh sibh |
| 3. cheanglódh sé | cheanglóidís | dhíbreodh sé | dhíbreoidís |
| *Autonomous* | | *Autonomous* | |
| cheanglófaí | | dhíbreofaí | |

## Present Subjunctive

| ceanglaím (ceangail) I tie | | díbrím (díbir) I banish | |
|---|---|---|---|
| *Sing.* | *Pl.* | *Sing.* | *Pl.* |
| 1. ceanglaí mé | ceanglaímid | díbrí mé | díbrímid |
| 2. ceanglaí tú | ceanglaí sibh | díbrí tú | díbrí sibh |
| 3. ceanglaí sé | ceanglaí siad | díbrí sé | díbrí siad |
| *Autonomous* | | *Autonomous* | |
| ceanglaítear | | díbrítear | |

## Imperative

| ceanglaím (ceangail) I tie | | díbrím (díbir) I banish | |
|---|---|---|---|
| *Sing.* | *Pl.* | *Sing.* | *Pl.* |
| 1. ceanglaím | ceanglaímis | díbrím | díbrímis |
| 2. ceangail | ceanglaígí | díbir | díbrígí |
| 3. ceanglaíodh sé | ceanglaídís | díbríodh sé | díbrídís |
| *Autonomous* | | *Autonomous* | |
| ceanglaítear | | díbrítear | |

## Verbal Noun

| ceanglaím (ceangail) I tie | díbrím (díbir) I banish |
|---|---|
| ceangal | díbirt |

## Verbal Adjective

| ceanglaím (ceangail) I tie | díbrím (díbir) I banish |
|---|---|
| ceangailte | díbeartha |

**EXERCISE**

We will banish the dictator. **Díbreoimid an deachtóir.**

How would you say: "I would banish the dictator?" You must go to the Conditional, first person singular: **Dhíbreoinn an deachtóir.** Obviously, there's a condition involved. "I would banish the dictator if ... I were in charge of the army ..." Anyway, we're all in agreement that he should go. So, how do we say: "Let us banish the dictator!" Go to the Imperative, first person plural: **Díbrímis an deachtóir!**

The verbal adjective tells us he's banished: **díbeartha.** Serves him right; he was an oppressor of minority languages ...

You have seen how verbs behave in Irish. Now let us revise what we have learned.


**VERB REVISION**

*1ˢᵗ Conjugation*

Verbs with one syllable, for example **mol**. Similarly: **buail** hit; **caill** lose; **can** sing; **cas** turn; **líon** fill; **rith** run; **scríobh** write; **scuab** brush.

Verbs with stems of more than one syllable, ending in -áil, for example **sábháil**. Similarly **bácáil** bake; **cniotáil** knit; **tástáil** test.

Verbs with stems of one syllable ending in -igh, for example **dóigh**. Similarly **báigh** drown; **brúigh** press; **glaoigh** call; **léigh** read; **nigh** wash; **suigh** sit.


*2ⁿᵈ Conjugation*

Verbs of two syllables or more, ending in -igh or -aigh, as in examples **beannaigh** and **cruinnigh**. Similarly: **ceannaigh** buy; **imigh** go; **éirigh** rise; **clúdaigh** cover; **tosaigh** begin; **smaoinigh** think; **fiafraigh** ask; **scrúdaigh** examine.

Syncopated verbs of more than one syllable, ending in **-il, -in, -ir, -is**, as in **ceangail, díbir**. Similarly: **codail** sleep; **bagair** threaten; **fógair** announce; **inis** relate (tell); **labhair** speak; **eitil** fly; **aithin** recognize. Also verbs of more than one syllable which are not syncopated: **foghlaim** learn; **taisteal** travel.

# Lesson 8: Professions

Laoise goes to a fortune-teller (bean feasa) to see what is in store for her.

Bean feasa:  **Beidh tú ag obair le do lámha.**
            You will be working with your hands.
Laoise:      **Tá sé sin an-ghinearálta, nach bhfuil? Bíonn máinlia ag obair lena lámha. Agus suathaire.**
            That's very general, isn't it? A surgeon works with his hands. As does a masseuse.
Bean feasa:  **Ceardaí a bheidh ionat.**
            You will be a craftsperson.
Laoise:      **Dáiríre?**
            Really?
Bean feasa:  **Bhfuil taithí ar bith ar cheardaíocht agat?**
            Have you any experience of craftwork?
Laoise:      **Dheisigh mé cathaoir uair amháin!**
            I once repaired a chair.
Bean feasa:  **Déantóir bréagán a bheidh ionat!**
            You will be a toy maker!
Laoise:      **Bréagáin?**
            Toys?
Bean feasa:  **Is ea ... bréagáin adhmaid.**
            Yes ... wooden toys.
Laoise:      **Bhuel, cé a shamhlódh é!**
            Well, who would imagine it!

## VOCABULARY

| | |
|---|---|
| accountant | **cuntasóir** (account = **cuntas**) |
| actor | **aisteoir** |
| anthropologist | **antrapeolaí** |
| archaeologist | **seandálaí** |

| | |
|---|---|
| architect | **ailtire** |
| astrologer | **astralaí** |
| athlete | **lúthchleasaí** |
| baby sitter | **feighlí** |
| baker | **báicéir** |
| banker | **baincéir** |
| biologist | **bitheolaí** |
| boatwright | **saor bád** |
| botanist | **luibheolaí** (herb = **luibh**) |
| boxer | **dornálaí** |
| builder | **tógálaí** |
| butcher | **búistéir** |
| carpenter | **siúinéir** |
| chef | **príomhchócaire** |
| cleaner | **glantóir** (clean = **glan** *v., adj.*) |
| cobbler | **gréasaí bróg** |
| composer | **cumadóir** (to compose = **cum**) |
| craftsperson | **ceardaí** |
| dancer | **rinceoir** (dance = **rince,** from English word "ring") also **damhsóir** (from Norman-French) |
| designer | **dearthóir** (to design = **dear**) |
| detective | **bleachtaire** |
| director/conductor | **stiúrthóir** |
| disc jockey | **diosceachaí** (steed = **each,** rider/jockey = **eachaí**) |
| doctor | **dochtúir** |
| driver | **tiománaí** |
| ecologist | **éiceolaí** |
| editor | **eagarthóir** |
| electrician | **leictreoir** |
| engineer | **innealtóir** |
| farmer | **feirmeoir** (**feilméara** in Connaught) |
| football player | **peileadóir** |
| gardener | **garraíodóir** |
| historian | **staraí** (history = **stair**) |
| hosteller | **tábhairneoir** |
| hurler | **iománaí** |
| jeweller | **seodóir** (jewel = **seoid**) |

| | |
|---|---|
| journalist | **iriseoir** |
| judge | **breitheamh** |
| lawyer | **dlíodóir** |
| lecturer | **léachtóir** |
| librarian | **leabharlannaí** |
| manager | **bainisteoir** |
| mechanic | **meicneoir** |
| milkman | **fear an bhainne** |
| model (fashion) | **mainicín** |
| musician | **ceoltóir** |
| nurse | **altra** (female form: **banaltra**) |
| pharmacist | **cógaseolaí** |
| philosopher | **fealsúnaí** |
| plumber | **pluiméir** |
| policeman | **garda** (in the Republic of Ireland) |
| policeman | **póilín** (outside of the Republic of Ireland) |
| politician | **polaiteoir** (politics = **polaitíocht**) |
| postman/woman | **fear/bean an phoist** |
| presenter | **láithreoir** |
| priest | **sagart** |
| psychiatrist | **síciatraí** |
| publisher | **foilsitheoir** |
| rabbi | **raibí** |
| receptionist | **fáilteoir** |
| scientist | **eolaí** |
| shepherd | **aoire** |
| singer | **amhránaí** (song = **amhrán**) |
| soldier | **saighdiúir** |
| tailor | **táilliúir** |
| teacher | **múinteoir** |
| theologian | **diagaire** |
| traffic warden | **maor tráchta** |
| turf accountant (bookie) | **geallghlacadóir** |
| veterinary surgeon | **tréidlia** |
| waiter | **freastalaí** |
| wrestler | **iomrascálaí** |
| writer | **scríbhneoir** |
| zoologist | **zó-eolaí** |

## GRAMMAR

### *The Prefixes "an-" and "ró"*

An- is a hyphenated intensive prefix which lenites the initial consonants b, c, f, g, m, p. It is pronounced **ana** in Munster.

Examples of **an-** with adjective:

| | |
|---|---|
| **Ceoltóirí an-bhreá iad.** | They are very fine musicians. |
| **Cathair an-mhór is ea í.** | It is a very big city. |
| **Duine an-deas is ea é.** | He is a very nice person. |

Examples of **an-** with noun:

| | |
|---|---|
| **An-chluiche ab ea é.** | It was a great game. |
| **Bhí an-teannas eatarthu.** | There was great tension between them. |

**Ró** does not hyphenate, except before a vowel:

| | |
|---|---|
| **Tá an gúna rótheann uirthi**. | The dress is too tight on her. |

# Lesson 9: Telling a Story

### DIALOGUE STUDY

We now look at an extended piece of dialogue in Munster Irish, a rarely seen piece from a book with the title *Cogar Mogar* by Diarmuid Ua Laoghaire, published in 1909.

One of the arguments during the early years of Conradh na Gaeilge (The Gaelic League) was whether to use the Irish of the Counter-Reformationist, Geoffrey Keating, as a literary model, or **caint na ndaoine** "the 'speech of the people'." The common speech won the day, but it is a speech uncommonly rich in color and idiomatic speech.

The following piece is worth studying along with the translation and comments.

**Diarmuid ag insint scéil dá chlainn.**
Diarmuid telling a story to his family.

Diarmuid: **Bailígí timpeall orm anois, a chlann ó, go neosfaidh mé scéal daoibh. Is fada dhom ag cuimhneamh ar é a insint daoibh ach níor fhéadas é go dtí so.**

Diarmuid: Gather round me now, dear children, until I tell you a story. I'm a long time thinking of telling it to you but I've been unable to up till now.

Cáit: **Cad ina thaobh, a Dhiarmuid?**
Cáit: Why is that, Diarmuid?

Máire: **Cad ina thaobh, a Dhiarmuid?! Mhuise féach air sin! Ba chóir go dtuigfeá féin cad ina thaobh agus gan a bheith ár mbodhradh.**

| | |
|---|---|
| Máire: | Why is that, Diarmuid?! Well, would you look at that! You yourself should know why and not be bothering us. |
| Cáit: | **An dtuigenn tusa cad ina thaobh, a Mháire?** |
| Cáit: | Do you know why, Máire? |
| Máire: | **Tuigim go hálainn andaighe. Cad ina thaobh ná tuigfinn? Agus do thuigfeása, leis, dá mbeadh aon tuiscint ionat, ach níl.** |
| Máire: | Indeed, I understand perfectly. Why wouldn't I understand? And you would understand as well if you had any understanding, but you haven't. |
| Cáit: | **Ós agatsa atá an insint go léir más ea, freagair mo cheistse.** |
| Cáit: | Since you have all the understanding so, answer my question. |
| Máire: | **Cad í an cheist?** |
| Máire: | What is the question? |
| Cáit: | **Cad ina thaobh nár inis Diarmuid an scéal dúinn fadó riamh?** |
| Cáit: | Why didn't Diarmuid tell us the story long before? |
| Máire: | **Mar níl sé ceaptha ar aon fhocal den fhírinne a insint dúinn agus ní raibh an bhréag curtha le chéile aige go dtí so.** |
| Máire: | Because he doesn't intend to tell us a word of the truth and he hadn't put the lie together before now. |
| Éamonn: | **Is sibh an bheirt chailíní is drochmhúinte dá bhfaca fós riamh im shúilibh cinn.** |
| Éamonn: | You are the two most ill-mannered girls I've ever laid eyes on. |
| Cáit: | **Conas san, a Éamoinn?** |
| Cáit: | How is that, Éamonn? |

Éamonn: **Conas san, a Éamoinn?! Mhuise, ar airigh éinne riamh a leithéid de cheist! Dá mbeadh aon urraim agaibh don té atá chun an scéil a insint dúinn, do scaoilfeadh sibh leis agus do ligfeadh sibh dó é a insint.**

Éamonn: How is that, Éamonn?! Well, did anyone ever hear such a question! If ye had respect for the one about to tell us the story, you'd allow him to proceed to tell it.

Cáit: **Agus cé tá ag moilliú an scéil?**

Cáit: And who is delaying the story?

Éamonn: **Cé tá ag moilliú an scéil? Andaigh mar a bhfuil fhios agatsa é ní fheadarsa cé aige go bhfuil fhios é.**

Éamonn: Who is delaying the story? Indeed, if you don't know it I don't know who does.

Cáit: **Ní mise tá á mhoilliú pé in Éirinn é.**

Cáit: I'm not delaying it anyway.

Éamonn: **Agus cé tá á mhoilliú mar sin?**

Éamonn: And who's delaying it so?

Cáit: **Tusa agus Máire.**

Cáit: Yourself and Máire.

Máire: **Bíodh geall anois go bhfuil Máire, leis, ciontach. Nuair atá botún déanta agat féin, ní foláir leat mise a tharrac isteach ann leis.**

Máire: You can bet, now, that Máire is to blame as well. When you've made a mistake yourself, you have to drag me into it as well.

Cáit: **Cad é an botún atá déanta agam, a Mháire? Ní thuigim féin go bhfuil aon bhotún déanta agam.**

Cáit: What's the mistake I've made, Máire? I don't understand myself that I've made any mistake.

Máire: **Tá fhios agamsa ná tuigeann tú. Dar ndóigh, dá dtuigfeá ní dhéanfá é. Nach cuimhin leat go ndúrt leat ná raibh aon tuiscint ionat? An cuimhin?**

| Máire: | I know you don't understand. Indeed, if you did understand you wouldn't have done it. Do you not remember that I told you that you had no understanding? Do you remember? |
|---|---|
| Cáit: | **Ní cuimhin.** |
| Cáit: | I don't. |
| Máire: | **An cuimhin leatsa é, a Éamoinn?** |
| Máire: | Do you remember it, Éamonn? |
| Éamonn: | **Is cuimhin.** |
| Éamonn: | I do. |
| Cáit: | **Féach anois tú, a Mháire, cad tá le rá agat?** |
| Cáit: | There you are now Máire, what do you have to say? |
| Máire: | **Tá a lán le rá agam dá ligfeása dhom é, ach ní ligfeá. Dúrt leatsa —** |
| Máire: | I've a lot to say, if you'd let me, but you won't. I told you — |
| Cáit: | **Tá a lán le rá agat dá ligfinnse dhuit é! Nílimse i do stop ar do rogha rud a rá, pé duine atá i do stop air.** |
| Cáit: | You've a lot to say if I'd let you! I'm not stopping you saying whatever you want to say, whoever else is stopping you. |
| Máire: | **Cé stop anois díreach mé?** |
| Máire: | Who stopped me just now? |
| Éamonn: | **Cáit gan amhras. Is é a bhí agam á rá ó chianaibh —** |
| Éamonn: | Cáit of course. What I was saying a while ago — |
| Cáit: | **Éist liom go fóill, a Éamoinn, ní ag teacht romhat ar do scéal é —** |
| Cáit: | Listen to me, a while, Éamonn, I'm not interrupting your story – |
| Éamonn: | **Cad eile ach ag teacht romham ar mo scéal! Dá mba áil leat gan teacht romham ar mo scéal ní bheadh aon ní** |

agam le tabhairt i do choinnibh; ach nuair a thánaís
romham ar mo scéal tá dhá ní agam le tabhairt i do
choinnibh, teacht romham ar mo scéal ar dtús, agus
ansan a rá nach ag teacht romham ar mo scéal a bhís.

Éamonn:     What else but interrupting my story! If you wished not to
            interrupt my story I wouldn't have two things to accuse
            you of, firstly interrupting my story, and then telling me
            that it was not interrupting my story you were.

Cáit:       **Seo, seo! Ní fearra dhúinn rud a dhéanfaimís ná éirí as
            an gclampar. Tosnaigh ar do scéal, a Dhiarmuid ...**
Cáit:       Now, now! We had best give up this wrangling. Start on
            your story, Diarmuid ...


## GRAMMAR NOTES

The title is **Ag insint scéil** "Telling a story".
**Scéal** is the nominative form; **insint** is the verbal noun of the verb **inis**.
**Ag** and the verbal noun will take the genitive. **Ag insint** also takes the
preposition **do**, or the pronoun forms: **dom, duit, dó, di, dúinn, daoibh,
dóibh**.

**Bhí mé ag insint scéil di.** "I was telling her a story."
**Dá** is a compound of the preposition **do** and the possessive adjective **a**.
**Dá chlainn** "to his family." This is a dative form of **clann** "family." The
standard written form would be **dá chlann** — the dative is dropped.

**Timpeall** can be a noun, preposition or, as here, a prepositional phrase
with the preposition **ar**, the pronoun forms of which are **orm, ort, air,
uirthi, orainn, oraibh, orthu. Cuir sreangán timpeall air** "put a string
around it."

**Ó** is part of an exclamatory phrase: **a chlann ó** "my dear family." We
find it in the song, *Fill, fill, a rún ó* ("Return, return my beloved").

**Neosfaidh** is a variant form of **inseoidh**, future of **inis**.

**Níor fhéadas** "I was not able." The root of this auxiliary verb is **féad**.
**Níor fhéadas** could also be expressed as **níor fhéad mé**.

**Cad ina thaobh** is also written **canathaobh** "why?" A smart answer to that might be **Gach aon taobh** "That is why," literally "every single side."

**Muise**, or **mhaise**, or **mhuise** is the Hiberno-English **musha** or **wisha**, meaning "indeed." Also written as **muis**. It is actually a corruption of **Muire**, "the Virgin Mary." One finds corrupt or veiled forms of "by Christ" in **dar cníops** and **dar príost**. Such corruptions are not peculiar to Irish: **zounds!** is "God's wounds!"

**Ár mbodhradh** or, more commonly, **ár mbodhrú**, means "bothering us." **Bodhraigh** is the verb "to deafen" or "to bother" and the English and Irish words are related. **Ná bí do mo bhodhrú** "don't bother me (bore me/annoy me)."

**Tusa** is the emphatic pronoun "you."

**Tuigim go hálainn**, literally: "I understand beautifully." Hiberno-English, "do you twig?" is the verb **tuig** "to understand" and "do you dig?" is probably **an dtuigeann tú?** as well!

**Go dtí so** "until now" or more commonly **go dtí seo**.

**An bheirt chailíní** "the two girls." **Beirt** is "two people" or "two things" in Ulster Irish. **Beirt** lenites, or softens with an **h**, and is followed by the genitive plural: **beirt mhac** "two sons."

**Drochmhúinte** is "ill-mannered" literally, "badly taught." **Im shúilibh cinn** is literally "in the eyes of my head," more commonly **le mo shúile cinn**. **Cinn** is the genitive of **ceann**.

**Dá scaoilfeadh sibh leis ... do ligfeadh sibh dó é a insint: do** is a verbal particle, usually omitted in the standard written form, though always included with verbs beginning with a vowel or **f: d'ólfainn an tSionainn** "I would drink the Shannon"; **d'fhreagair tú mo cheist** "you answered my question."

**Pé in Éirinn é** "Whoever it might be." **Pé** is a pronoun, adjective and conjunction, meaning "whoever" and **in Éirinn**, literally "in Ireland," using the dative form of **Éire**.

**Cé tá** is more commonly written **cé atá**.

**A tharrac** is more commonly written **a tharraingt**.

**Tá fhios agamsa ná tuigeann tú** would read in the standardized form: **Tá a fhios agamsa nach dtuigeann tú**.

**Go ndúrt leat** could also be written **go ndúirt mé leat**.

**Is é a bhí agam á rá** is more commonly constructed as **is é a bhí á rá agam**. The vowels slide into one another so that **is é a bhí** would be voiced **sé bhí** (pronounced *shay vee*).

**I do choinnibh** "against you" more commonly written **i do choinne**. **Thánaís** "you came" commonly written, outside Munster, as **tháinig tú**. **Thánaís romham** "you came before me" or "interrupted me." **Bhís = bhí tú** "you were."

# Lesson 10: Do Me A Favor

Laoise and Seosamh are in a café.

Laoise:    **Déan rud <u>orm</u>!**
           Do me a favor!
Seosamh:   **Cinnte.**
           Sure.
Laoise:    **Can amhrán <u>dom</u>!**
           Sing me a song!
Seosamh:   **An <u>as</u> do mheabhair atá tú? Ní chanfainn amhrán <u>ar</u> ór na**
           **cruinne.**
           Are you mad? I wouldn't sing a song for all the money in
           the world.
Laoise:    **Cén fáth nach gcanfá amhrán <u>dom</u>?**
           Why wouldn't you sing a song for me?
Seosamh:   **Caithfidh mé tabhairt <u>faoin</u> oifig. Tá se a deich <u>chun</u> a dó.**
           I'll have to be heading for the office. It's ten to two ...
Laoise:    **Feicfidh mé <u>um</u> thráthnóna thú.**
           I'll see you tonight.

## THE BUILDING BLOCKS OF IRISH

Prepositions such as **roimh, le, faoi,** etc. form the building blocks of
Irish. Study the examples in this section, over and over again, and you
will improve your oral and your written Irish!

This is the first Irish language primer for beginners to emphasize the
importance of these small words that go a long way!

**FAOI** : **fúm, fút, faoi, fúithi, fúinn, fúibh, fúthu** - with **an** = **faoin.**

- **Amuigh faoin spéir.** Out in the open (i.e. under the sky).
- **Chuaigh sí i bhfolach faoin mbord.** She hid under the table.
- **Cuir líne faoi.** Underline it.
- **Bhí an ghrian ag dul faoi.** The sun was setting.
- **Ag lorg an chapaill bháin is an capall bán fút.** Looking for the white horse and the white horse under you (i.e. mounted on the white horse).
- **Fiche bliain faoi bhláth.** Twenty years a-blooming.
- **Coinnigh an páiste sin faoi smacht.** Keep that child under control.
- **Bhí an-luas fúthu.** They were going at great speed.
- **Buail fút!** Sit down! (take a seat).
- **Tá na caoirigh faoi shneachta.** The sheep are buried in snow.
- **Chuir sé faoi i Manchain.** He settled down in Manchester.
- **Tá borradh an éin gé fúithi.** She is growing rapidly (like a young goose).
- **Mise faoi duit!** I assure you!
- **Cad faoi atá sé?** What's it about?
- **Faoi mar a shlogfadh an talamh é!** As though the earth swallowed him!
- **Cuireadh faoi scian aréir í.** She was operated on last night.
- **Dúirt mé leat faoi dhó é.** I told you twice.
- **A sé faoi a sé.** Six by six.
- **Tríocha faoin gcéad.** Thirty per cent.
- **Níl aon Ghaeilge thart faoi seo.** There's no Irish around here.
- **Tá mé an-imníoch fút.** I'm very concerned about you.
- **Tháinig siad faoi dheireadh.** They came at last.
- **Thug mé fogha faoi.** I lunged at him.
- **Níl aon duine ann faoi láthair.** There's no one there at the moment.
- **Ní aontóinn leat faoi sin.** I wouldn't agree with you about that.
- **Fúmsa atá sé anois.** It's up to me now.
- **Chuir sí an t-airgead faoi ghlas.** She locked away the money.
- **Ba chóir go mbeadh sé ann faoi seo.** It should be there by now.
- **Faoi sholas an lae a tharla sé.** It happened in daylight.
- **Bhí Fionn bocht faoi gheasa aici.** Poor Fionn was under her spell. (In Ulster you often find **fá** instead of **faoi**: **Cad é atá tú ag caint fá dtaobh de?** "What are you talking about?")

**DE: díom, díot, de, di, dínn, díbh, díobh;** with **an - den**.

- **Bain an leabhar sin di.** Take that book from her.
- **Tá an cupán greamaithe den bhord.** The cup is stuck to the table.
- **Laistiar den teach atá an leithreas.** The toilet is behind the house.
- **Duine de lucht RTE í sin.** She's one of the RTE crowd.
- **Ceannaigh earraí de dhéantús na hÉireann.** Buy Irish-made goods.
- **Cailleadh den tart í.** She died of thirst.
- **A leithéid de sheafóid!** Such rubbish!
- **Níl ach cuid bheag den airgead fágtha.** There's only a small amount of the money left.
- **Thit Micheál den chapall.** Micheál fell off the horse.
- **Cuir an dán sin de ghlanmheabhair.** Learn that poem off by heart.
- **Bíonn sí ag gearán d'oíche agus de lá.** She never stops complaining (by night and by day).
- **Bhí sé de nós acu paidir a rá roimh dhul a luí.** It was customary with them to say a prayer before going to bed.
- **Táim bréan de!** I'm fed up with it!
- **De réir an tseanchais.** According to tradition.

**LE: liom, leat, leis/léi, linn, libh, leo.**

- **Féach anois mé is mo chúl le balla.** Look at me now with my back to the wall.
- **Cuir srian le do theanga!** Control your tongue!
- **Thugas mo chúl leo.** I turned my back on them.
- **Tá mé ag súil go mór le mo lá breithe.** I'm greatly looking forward to my birthday.
- **Ná caith le haill é!** Don't throw it away!
- **Cónaím anois liom féin.** I live alone now.
- **Bhí an t-ádh leat, a bhuachaill!** You were lucky, boy!
- **Dia go deo linn!** God bless us!
- **Iníon léi is ea Bríd.** Bríd is a daughter of hers.
- **Bhí an t-ádh dearg léi!** She was really lucky!
- **Ní haon mhaith a bheith leo.** There's no point in being at them. (It's no good trying to convince them.)
- **Leis sin.** Thereupon.
- **Le mo linn féin.** During my own time (lifetime).
- **I gcomparáid le Síle.** Compared with Síle.
- **Chomh dubh le pic.** As black as pitch.
- **Imigh leat anois!** Off with you now!

- **Le do thoil.** If you please.
- **Bhí dán léi ar an bpáipéar scrúdaithe.** There was a poem by her on the exam paper.
- **Chuaigh sé le báiní ar fad!** He went crazy!
- **Bhí sé ag léim as a chraiceann le háthas.** He was jumping out of his skin with joy.
- **Le greann a dúirt sí é.** She said it only in jest.
- **Is dóigh liom go bhfuil an ceart agat.** I think you're right.
- **Bí cineálta léi.** Be kind to her.
- **Labhróidh mé leat amárach.** I'll talk to you tomorrow.
- **Ní aontóinn leat!** I wouldn't agree with you.
- **Níl faic le rá aige.** He has nothing to say.

**AR: orm, ort, air/uirthi, orainn, oraibh, orthu.**

- **D'imigh sé ar cosa in airde.** He went off at a gallop.
- **Tá sé ar fáil ar cíos.** It's available to rent.
- **Ar muir is ar tír.** On sea and on land.
- **Chuaigh sí ar a glúine.** She went on her knees.
- **Bhí an long ar ancaire sa chuan.** The ship was anchored in the harbor.
- **Cá bhfuil tú ar scoil?** Where do you go to school?
- **Tá sé ar dhuine de na scríbhneoirí is spéisiúla sa tír.** He is one of the most interesting writers in the country.
- **A grua ar dhath an róis.** Her cheek the color of a rose.
- **Leath a cáil ar fud Chiarraí.** Her fame spread throughout Kerry.
- **Bhí sé ar leathshúil.** He had only one eye.
- **Ní scarfainn leis ar ór na cruinne.** I wouldn't part with it for all the gold in the world.
- **Ar m'anam!** Upon my soul!
- **Chuaigh sé ar oilithreacht go Meice.** He went on a pilgrimage to Mecca.
- **Ar m'éirí dom ar maidin.** When I got up in the morning.
- **Tá dea-chuma air.** It looks good.
- **Cuir ort do hata.** Put on your hat.
- **Níl aon ráchairt air.** There's no demand for it.
- **Ortsa an milleán!** You're to blame!
- **Tá an ghráin agam ar mheisceoirí.** I hate drunkards.
- **Tá tart orm.** I'm thirsty.
- **Cén diabhal atá ort!** What the devil is wrong with you!
- **Tá deich bpunt agam air.** He owes me ten pounds.

- **Ná bí ag ligean ort!** Don't be pretending!
- **Ná tabhair aon aird uirthi!** Don't mind her!
- **Shatail siad orm.** They trampled on me.
- **Seinneann sí ar an bpianó.** She plays the piano.
- **Theip air.** He failed.
- **Cuir glao orm.** Give me a ring.
- **Tá an Ghaeilge imithe sa chloigeann air.** Irish has gone to his head.

**I: ionam, ionat, ann, inti, ionainn, ionaibh, iontu.**

- **I measc na bplód gan ainm.** Among the crowds without a name.
- **Tá sí i bhfad ó bhaile anois.** She's far from home now.
- **Cé atá i bhfeighil na bpáistí?** Who is minding the children?
- **Níl tú i bpian, an bhfuil?** You're not in pain, are you?
- **Chuir sí a toil i bhfeidhm orm.** She imposed her will on me.
- **Bhí Heloïse i ngrá le hAbélard.** Heloïse was in love with Abelard.
- **Cé atá i gcumhacht sa tír sin?** Who is in power in that country?
- **Scríobhfaidh mé chugat i gceann seachtaine.** I'll write to you in a week.
- **Labhair i gceart!** Speak properly!
- **Níl aon mhaith ionat!** You're no good!
- **File maith a bhí inti.** She was a good poet.
- **Níl iontu ach paca bligeard!** They're only a crowd of blackguards!
- **Cuir i do mhála é.** Put it in your bag.
- **Tá sé ag dul i bhfeabhas.** He's improving.
- **Creidim i nDia an tAthair Uilechumhachtach.** I believe in God the Father Almighty.

**IDIR: eadrainn, eadraibh, eatarthu.**

- **Ná bí ag ithe idir bhéilí!** Don't be eating between meals!
- **Idir Doire agus Béal Feirste.** Between Derry and Belfast.
- **Ceannaímis eadrainn é.** Let's buy it between us.
- **Eadrainn féin é seo.** This is between ourselves.
- **Is beannaithe thú idir mhná.** Blessed art thou among women.
- **Bíonn idir fhir agus mhná ann.** Both men and women frequent the place.
- **Idir shúgradh is dáiríre.** Half in jest, half in earnest.
- **Tá mé idir dhá chomhairle.** I'm between two minds.

## REVISION: SOME USES OF PREPOSITIONS

The building blocks are called prepositions. They can describe:

Substance

**Déanta de chopar a bhí sé.** It was made of copper.

Time

| | |
|---|---|
| **ar ball** | soon |
| **Ar a cúig a chlog ar maidin.** | At five o'clock in the morning. |
| **Idir an Nollaig agus an Cháisc.** | Between Christmas and Easter. |
| **A cúig chun a cúig.** | Five to five. |
| **Tar chugam roimh am lóin.** | Come to me before lunchtime. |
| **Níor labhair sé focal as sin amach.** | He never spoke a word after that. |
| **Thit sé sin go léir amach le mo linn féin.** | All that happened in my lifetime. |

Origin

| | |
|---|---|
| **An as an nGearmáin é Hans?** | Is Hans from Germany? |
| **Cá bhfuair tú an chíor? Ó mo mháthair a fuaireas í.** | Where did you get the comb? I got it from my mother. |

Exclusion

| | |
|---|---|
| **Ní raibh aon duine ann ach mé féin!** | I was the only one there! |
| **Spéir gan réiltín, tinteán gan leanbh.** | A sky without a little star, a home without a child. |
| **Cá mbeinn murach í?** | Where would I be without her? |
| **Is bréagadóirí iad go léir seachas Maidhc.** | They're all liars except for Maidhc. |
| **Thar éinne eile cé a shiúlfadh isteach ach...?** | Who of all people should walk in but...? |

Plural

**Léigh an leathanach seo faoi dhó.** Read this page twice.

Method

**As Béarla a bhí na fógraí scoile go léir.**
All the school notices were in English.

**D'fharraige a chuaigh sí ann.**
She went there by sea.

**I nGaeilge uasal cheolmhar a labhair sí liom.**
She spoke to me in noble, melodious Irish.

Comparison

**Bhí Jack Charlton níos fearr ná Mick McCarthy.**
Jack Charlton was better than Mick McCarthy.

Cause

**Cuireadh i bpríosún é as teilifíseán a ghoid.**
He was imprisoned for stealing a television set.

**Bhí sí ag damhsa le háthas!**
She was dancing with joy!

**Cailleadh den ocras iad.**
They died of hunger.

**Táim bodhar ó bheith ag éisteacht léi!**
I'm deaf from listening to her!

Selling and Buying

**Cad a thug tú ar an gcasóg?**
What did you pay for the jacket?

**Níl mé in ann íoc as.**
I can't pay for it.

**Dhíolas na físeáin le Caitríona.**
I sold the videos to Caitríona.

**Tá caint saor agus airgead ar thobac.**
Talk is free and you've to pay for tobacco.

Exclamation

**Dar m'fhocal!**
Upon my word!

**Dar m'anam!**
Upon my soul!

**Ar mo leabhar breac!**
On my solemn oath!

## Position

| | |
|---|---|
| Léigh mé ar COMHAR é. | I read it in COMHAR. |
| Is gaoth ar muir mé. | I am the wind on the sea. |
| In Éirinn a rugadh í. | She was born in Ireland. |
| Tá Tír na nÓg ar chúl an tí. | The Land of Youth is behind the house. |
| Stop an t-asal os comhair an tí. | The donkey stopped in front of the house. |
| Áit éigin idir Cill Mocheallóg agus Cill Fhíonáin. | Somewhere between Kilmallock and Kilfinane. |
| Fiche míle ó Bhaile Bhuirne. | Twenty miles from Baile Bhuirne. |

## Movement (from)

| | |
|---|---|
| Seo linn as seo in ainm Dé! | Let's get out of here in the name of God! |
| Chuaigh mé ó theach go teach. | I went from house to house. |

## Movement (towards)

| | |
|---|---|
| Nach bhfuil tú ag dul ar scoil inniu? | Are you not going to school today? |
| An mbeidh tú ag dul go dtí an dioscó anocht? | Will you be going to the disco tonight? |
| Tháinig mo ghrása | My love came |
| Le mo thaobh | To my side |
| Gualainn ar ghualainn | Shoulder to shoulder |
| Agus béal ar bhéal. | And mouth to mouth. |
| Ní rachainn chuig an gcóisir leatsa! | I wouldn't go to the party with you! |
| Báidín Fhélimí d'imigh go Gabhla. | Féilimí's boat went to Gabhla. |
| Chuaigh scata acu thar sáile. | A lot of them went abroad. |
| Rachaidh mé faoin gcoill leat. | I'll go to the wood with you. |
| Shiúil sí trasna na sráide. | She walked across the street. |

Inclusion

| | |
|---|---|
| **Bíonn idir fhir is mhná sa chlub.** | Both men and women frequent the club. |
| **Tá sí ar dhuine de na filí is fearr san Eoraip.** | She is one of the finest poets in Europe. |

Possession

| | |
|---|---|
| **Is le Síle an peann sin.** | That pen is Síle's. |
| **Mac liom a bhuaigh an corn.** | A son of mine won the cup. |
| **Níl pingin rua agam.** | I haven't a penny. |

Direction

| | |
|---|---|
| **D'iompaigh sí uaim.** | She turned away from me. |
| **Féach anois mé is mo chúl le Balla.** | Look at me now with my back to Balla. |
| **Caithfimid aghaidh a thabhairt ar an mbóthar abhaile.** | We'll have to be getting home. |

Qualification

| | |
|---|---|
| **Bhí an gadhar bocht ar leathchluas.** | The poor dog had only one ear. |
| **Fathach sé troithe ar airde is ea é.** | He's a six-foot high giant. |
| **Caoga punt faoi nó thairis.** | Fifty pounds more or less. |
| **Bhí sé thar am aici é a rá.** | It was time for her to say it. |

Condition

| | |
|---|---|
| **Tá mé ar buile leat.** | I'm mad with you. |
| **Ba cheart é a chur faoi ghlas.** | He should be locked up. |
| **Bhí sé ina chónaí i gCaiseal an uair úd.** | He lived in Cashel then. |
| **Bhí na deora léi.** | She was crying. |

## Curses

| | |
|---|---|
| **Diabhal agus daichead ort!** | A devil and forty of them on you! |
| **Codladh an traonaigh chugat!** | The corncrake's sleep to you! (i.e. Sleep the whole day, you lazy good-for-nothing!) |

## Blessings and Toasts

| | |
|---|---|
| **Is mór mo ghean ort!** | I'm very fond of you! |
| Answer: **Aithním sin ort!** | I can see that by you! |

## Emotions/Personal Condition

| | |
|---|---|
| **Tá fuacht orm.** | I'm cold. |
| **Tá tart orm.** | I'm thirsty. |
| **Tá imní uirthi.** | She's worried. |
| **Bhí eagla orainn.** | We were afraid. |

# Revisions

### Ag

| Sing. | Pl. |
|-------|-----|
| agam | againn |
| agat | agaibh |
| aige (*masc.*) | acu |
| aici (*fem.*) | |

### EXERCISE

How would you say: "She has no sense!"
**Níl aon chiall <u>aici</u>!**

How would you say: "They have no sense!"
**Níl aon chiall <u>acu</u>!**

(**Aon,** by the way, lenites, except before the letters **d,t,** and **s**)

### Ar

| Sing. | Pl. |
|-------|-----|
| orm | orainn |
| ort | oraibh |
| air (*masc.*) | orthu |
| uirthi (*fem.*) | |

**EXERCISE**

How would you say: "Are you thirsty?" (literally: Have you thirst on you?)
**An bhfuil tart ort?**

How would you say: "Is she thirsty?"
**An bhfuil tart uirthi?**

(In conversation, the interrogative verbal particle **an** is often dropped)

**As**

| Sing. | Pl. |
|---|---|
| asam | asainn |
| asat | asaibh |
| as (*masc.*) | astu |
| aisti (*fem.*) | |

**EXERCISE**

I have confidence in you. **Tá muinín agam asat.**

How would you say: "I have confidence in her"?
**Tá muinín agam aisti.**

How would you say: "I have confidence in them"?
**Tá muinín agam astu.**

**Chuig**

| Sing. | Pl. |
|---|---|
| chugam | chugainn |
| chugat | chugaibh |
| chuige (*masc.*) | chucu |
| chuici (*fem.*) | |

**EXERCISE**

I will write to her. **Scríobhfaidh mé chuici**.

How would you say: "I will write to you"?
**Scríobhfaidh mé chugat.**

How would you say: "Will you write to me?"
**An scríobhfaidh tú chugam?**

**De**

| Sing. | Pl. |
|---|---|
| díom | dínn |
| díot | díbh |
| de (*masc.*) | díobh |
| di (*fem.*) | |

**EXERCISE**

I am fed up with you. **Tá mé bréan díot!**

How would you say: "I am fed up with her!"
**Ta mé bréan di.**

**Do**

| Sing. | Pl. |
|---|---|
| dom | dúinn |
| duit | daoibh |
| dó (*masc.*) | dóibh |
| di (*fem.*) | |

**EXERCISE**

He gave it to me. **Thug sé <u>dom</u> é.**

How would you say: "She gave it to her"?
**Thug sí <u>di</u> é.**

How would you say: "I gave it to them"?
**Thug mé <u>dóibh</u> é.**

**Faoi**

| Sing. | Pl. |
|---|---|
| fúm | fúinn |
| fút | fúibh |
| faoi (*masc.*) | fúthu |
| fúithi (*fem.*) | |

**EXERCISE**

Do you intend to go? **An bhfuil <u>fút</u> imeacht?**

How would you say: "Do they intend to go?"
**An bhfuil <u>fúthu</u> imeacht?**

I

| Sing. | Pl. |
|---|---|
| ionam | ionainn |
| ionat | ionaibh |
| ann (*masc.*) | iontu |
| inti (*fem.*) | |

## EXERCISE

She is a good woman. **Bean mhaith atá <u>inti</u>.**

How would you say: "He is a good boy"?
**Buachaill maith atá <u>ann</u>.**

Le

| Sing. | Pl. |
|---|---|
| liom | linn |
| leat | libh |
| leis (*masc.*) | leo |
| léi (*fem.*) | |

## EXERCISE

I'll be with you (*sing.*) in a moment. **Beidh mé <u>leat</u> i gceann nóiméid.**

How would you say: "I'll be with you (*pl.*) in a moment"?
**Beidh mé <u>libh</u> i gceann nóiméid.**

# Ó

| Sing. | Pl. |
|---|---|
| uaim | uainn |
| uait | uaibh |
| uaidh (*masc.*) | uathu |
| uaithi (*fem.*) | |

## EXERCISE

What does he want? **Cad tá <u>uaidh</u>?**

How would you say: "What does she want?"
**Cad tá <u>uaithi</u>?**

## Roimh

| Sing. | Pl. |
|---|---|
| romham | romhainn |
| romhat | romhaibh |
| roimhe (*masc.*) | rompu |
| roimpi (*fem.*) | |

## EXERCISE

The whole world is ahead of her. **Tá an saol ar fad <u>roimpi</u>.**

How would you say: "The whole world is ahead of me"?
**Tá an saol ar fad <u>romham</u>.**

# *Other Irish interest titles from Hippocrene . . .*

**IRISH-ENGLISH/ENGLISH-IRISH DICTIONARY AND PHRASEBOOK**
This 1,400-word dictionary indicates pronunciation in English spelling and will swiftly acquaint visitors with a basic key vocabulary. Phrases cover travel, sightseeing, shopping, and recreation, and notes are provided on grammar, pronunciation, and dialect.
71 pages • 1,400 entries • 3¾ x 7 • ISBN 0-87052-110-1 • $7.95pb • (385)

**IRISH-ENGLISH/ENGLISH-IRISH PRACTICAL DICTIONARY**
20,000 entries comprise this handy dictionary, the newest title in Hippocrene's successful Irish library.
250 pages • 20,000 entries • 4 x 6½ • ISBN 0-7818-0777-8 • $12.95pb • (39)

**OGHAM: AN IRISH ALPHABET**
The form of Irish known as Ogham was established as a medium of written communication by the fourth century A.D. Ogham is believed to have been influenced by the Latin alphabet and consists of twenty letters each represented by one or more lines or notches carved along a vertical line, for example along the edge of a standing stone, as illustrated in this book. *Ogham: An Irish Alphabet* is a bilingual explanation and beautifully illustrated representation of the ancient and enigmatic Ogham alphabet.
60 pages • 5½ x 8½ • ISBN 0-7818-0665-8 • $7.95pb • (757)

**IRISH GRAMMAR: A BASIC HANDBOOK**
Students who are beginners, adults who need to brush up, or teachers in need of a trustworthy reference guide will welcome this handy, straightforward grammar handbook with its attractive format and easy-to-use approach.
The author Noel McGonagle is a lecturer in the Modern Irish Department of University College, Galway. He has written extensively on linguistic and literary aspects of Modern Irish.
100 pages • 5¼ x 7½ • ISBN 0-7818-0667-4 • $9.95pb • (759)

**IRISH PROVERBS**
Two hundred proverbs relate the hard times, the good times and the great times experienced by the Irish people. Thirty illustrations from County Sligo artist Fergus Lyons add style and humor to this collection of wit and wisdom in the great oral tradition of Ireland.
104 pages • 5½ x 8½ • 30 illustrations • ISBN 0-7818-0676-3 • $14.95pb • (761)

**HIPPOCRENE CHILDREN'S ILLUSTRATED IRISH DICTIONARY**
With 500 entries, this one of a kind dictionary is designed to engage children visually and to facilitate the acquisition of Irish language skills. Each word is accompanied by illustrations of objects and actions common to a child's everyday experience. An Irish-English glossary makes this an effective learning tool for non-English speakers as well.
94 pages • 500 entries • 9 x 11 • ISBN 0-7818-0713-1 • $14.95hc • (798)

**IRISH HUMOROUS POETRY**
191 pages • 5½ x 8½ • ISBN 0-7818-0745-X • $14.95pb • (56)

**IRELAND: AN ILLUSTRATED HISTORY**
166 pages • 50 illustrations • 5 x 7 • ISBN 0-7818-0693-3 • $11.95hc • (782)

All prices subject to change without prior notice. **To order Hippocrene Books** contact your local bookstore, call (718) 454-2366, or write to: Hippocrene Books, 171 Madison Avenue, New York, NY 10016. Please enclose check or money order, adding $5.00 shipping (UPS) for the first book and $.50 for each additional book.

**Thar**

| Sing. | Pl. |
|---|---|
| tharam | tharainn |
| tharat | tharaibh |
| thairis (*masc.*) | tharstu |
| thairsti (*fem.*) | |

## EXERCISE

I passed her by on the road. **Ghabh mé <u>thairsti</u> ar an mbóthar.**

How would you say: "You passed me by on the road"?
**Ghabh tú <u>tharam</u> ar an mbóthar.**